SARAH DALLAS

VINTAGE KNITS

First published in Great Britain in 2002
1 3 5 7 9 10 8 6 4 2

Text © Sarah Dallas 2002
Photographs © Catherine Gratwicke 2002

Ebury Press
Random House, 20 Vauxhall Bridge Road, London SW1V 2SA

Random House Australia (Pty) Limited
20 Alfred Street, Milsons Point, Sydney, New South Wales 2061, Australia

Random House New Zealand Limited
18 Poland Road, Glenfield, Auckland 10, New Zealand

Random House (Pty) Limited
Endulini, 5a Jubilee Road, Parktown 2193, South Africa

The Random House Group Limited Reg. No. 954009
www.randomhouse.co.uk

Papers used by Ebury Press are natural, recyclable products made from wood
grown in sustainable forests.

A CIP catalogue record for this book is available from the British Library

ISBN 0 09 187929 9

Editor EMMA CALLERY
Art director GEORGINA RHODES
Photographer CATHERINE GRATWICKE
Stylist FRANCINE KAY
Patterns compiled by EVA YATES
Patterns checked by MARILYN WILSON

Printed and bound in Singapore by Tien Wah Press

SARAH DALLAS

PHOTOGRAPHS BY CATHERINE GRATWICKE

VINTAGE KNITS

EBURY PRESS
LONDON

Contents

Introduction

The unique craft of knitting provides the wonderful, instantly satisfing experience of creating something with your own hands. You are in control from start to finish making the fabric and the garment in the same process from a thread of yarn.

The period spanning the 1940s and the 1950s continues to be a constant source of inspiration for the knitwear designer. This was a time when knitting was not only a hobby but a necessity and was one of the most available skills that enabled families to provide for themselves. All that was required was a ball of wool, knitting needles and some time.

Almost any article of clothing could be knitted; from underwear to sweaters, skirts, dresses, jackets, coats and accessories. And when worn out, they were unravelled and the yarn used again.

The ingenuity exhibited in some of these garments is quite extraordinary. The skill involved in the shaping and construction of a garment was extremely inventive. This was all-important at a time when the choice of yarn available was limited to a few qualities and in a minimum of colours, so the structures within the knit and the garment making itself were essential features, not only to produce what you wanted and needed, but also perhaps to exhibit certain skills and expertise. Detail and finish were paramount. These were fashionable garments.

It is these elements that have the integrity to endure the test of time and have been passed down and continually reworked for a modern and contemporary look in knitwear. The designs shown here have incorporated many of the details of the forties and fifties while using current yarns and colour combinations to take the ideas forward in a new and fresh direction. The inspiration for colour came from flowers to bring a united and cohesive look to the collection of knits and to add a spirit of joy.

Lace vest

SEE PATTERN ON PAGE 68

There's something very sexy about this ultra-feminine lacey knitted vest. Maybe it's the pattern of the pointelle knit, maybe it's the satin ribbon threaded through the pretty trim. Whatever the reason, it translates beautifully into an alluring little camisole top for modern living.

Cotton jacket with chenille edgings SEE PATTERN ON PAGE 70

There is a much wider range of yarns available now than during this period. The use of chenille
to edge this knitted cotton jacket adds texture and style to this very practical garment.

Short-sleeved fairisle sweater

PATTERN ON PAGE 72

Only small quantities of several colours of yarn were required to knit fairisle garments. Oddments of wool, never wasted, were gathered together to knit sweaters as shown in this up-to-the-minute short-sleeved fairisle sweater.

Long-sleeved cotton jacket SEE PATTERN ON PAGE 74

The shape of this button-through ribbed cardigan is reminiscent of a contemporary denim jacket and translates well into a casual, sporty separate.

Short-sleeved diamond stitch sweater

SEE PATTERN ON PAGE 76

Short-sleeved sweaters were the staple of most women's wardrobes. Women did not have the number or choice of clothes they have these days. They were trans-seasonal and could take a wardrobe through from winter to summer, as shown with this delicately textured little sweater.

Cable sweater SEE PATTERN ON PAGE 78

A cable takes up more yarn than stocking stitch. In the 1940s, few patterns incorporated cables as yarn was in short supply. Therefore cables were used sparingly as details.

Ribbed sweater

SEE PATTERN ON PAGE 80

Throughout the period, the emphasis in fashion was on a tiny waist. It was not unusual for women to have a waist of 21 inches or smaller. Knitting patterns used devices like this rib to accentuate the style.

Short-sleeved cardigan with bow

SEE PATTERN ON PAGE 82

When supplies of yarn wer scarce, particularly during the forties, worn-out sweater were unravelled and the wool re-used to make new garments, often using a stitch structure so that any imperfections in the reclaimed yarn were disguised.

Short-sleeved ribbed lace sweater PATTERN ON PAGE 84

Though part of a twinset (see the cardigan overleaf), this charming short-sleeved sweater with its pretty ribbed lace stitch works equally well worn on its own without the cardigan.

Long-sleeved ribbed cardigan

SEE PATTERN ON PAGE 86

There is now a greater choice of yarns available to the knitter, such as the linen mix yarn used to knit this twinset. A modern twist to the twinset is to knit the sweater in a contrasting colour to the cardigan.

Short-sleeved sweater with mohair stripe

SEE PATTERN ON PAGE 88

Novelty yarns were used sparingly but to great effect, as reflected in this stylish sweater.

Fluffy sweater

SEE PATTERN ON PAGE 90

This pretty sweater is simple
to knit and has enough detail
in the cabled ribs to make it
special. A mohair mix yarn
was chosen to keep the spirit
of the original design.

Long-sleeved striped sweater SEE PATTERN ON PAGE 92

This very graphic, modern design is created with larger blocks of coloured stripes
and the sharp contrast of thinner, more narrowly spaced burgundy coloured stripes.
A sophisticated design, which is nevertheless easy to knit.

Short-sleeved striped cotton sweater

SEE PATTERN ON PAGE 94

The development of new yarns in a wider and exciting choice of colours has inevitably broadened the scope for the knitwear designer. By updating the yarn and the colours this simple sweater looks very modern.

Mittens with cabled ribs

SEE PATTERN ON PAGE 96

Through the long, cold winters
it was essential to wrap up
warm. These mittens could be
knitted with odds and ends of
leftover yarn.

Lace cardigan

SEE PATTERN ON PAGE 98

The use of a contemporary yarn
such as the cotton used to knit
this cardigan really defines the
structure and enhances the look
to this lacey stitch.

Fairisle gloves and beret

SEE PATTERNS ON PAGES 100 AND 101

A pair of fairisle gloves and a matching beret — and matching was the vital word at this date. No woman considered herself to be well dressed unless her accessories — hat, shoes, gloves and handbag — all toned with each other, and with her outfit.

Cotton twinset

SEE PATTERN ON PAGES 102 AND 104

Twinsets were fashionable in the 1950s. The cardigan provided a smart yet less formal alternative to the tailored jacket. Suits, or tailormades as they were called, were both expensive to buy and difficult to make if you were a home dressmaker.

Short-sleeved lace sweater with ribbons

SEE PATTERN ON PAGE 106

The upswept hairstyle defines the original pattern as vintage. But this charming short-sleeved lace patterned sweater can look as modern today as it did fifty years ago when it was first knitted. Give it the personal touch by threading through different coloured ribbons to go with different skirts and trousers.

Short-sleeved wavy line sweater

SEE PATTERN ON PAGE 108

Knitting patterns and fashion photographs in magazines were mainly printed in black and white at this date. To give readers and knitters a good idea of the exact colours of a garment, copywriters used descriptive phrases such as, 'beech brown', pearl grey', 'china blue' and 'bird feather brown'.

Fairisle cardigan

SEE PATTERN ON PAGE 110

There was a strong desire to
look smart and be fashionable
during this period but
because of rationing it was
more economical to make
clothes than buy them.
Coupons could buy more
materials than finished
garments. Women put their
considerable skills in knitting
to good use and created
neat little garments like this
fairisle cardigan.

Silk ribbed vest

SEE PATTERN ON PAGE 114

Bizarre as it seems today even underwear was knitted in the mid-twentieth century. Knitted undies played an important role in keeping women warm. Most people did not have centrally-heated houses and few had their own cars, so had to wait at draughty bus stops or on icy station platforms. This vest has a new twist on the original version and is knitted in luxurious silk.

Long-sleeved bolero

SEE PATTERN ON PAGE 116

The shrug, the fashionable
garment of recent seasons,
in fact first hit the couture
showrooms in the early 1950s.
This bolero was a pretty party
version of the same style.

Striped socks and chequered scarf

SEE PATTERNS ON PAGES 118 AND 119

'Make do and mend' was the advice of the government to the population throughout the 1940s. Women were encouraged to patch and darn their clothes, make garments from curtains and use every last scrap of material or wool. Making a virtue out of necessity, knitters devised intricate patterns, using small quantities of yarn. No yarn was wasted. Very small amounts of mixed colours were used to knit accessories. These ankle socks provided warmth and comfort on cold chilly nights.

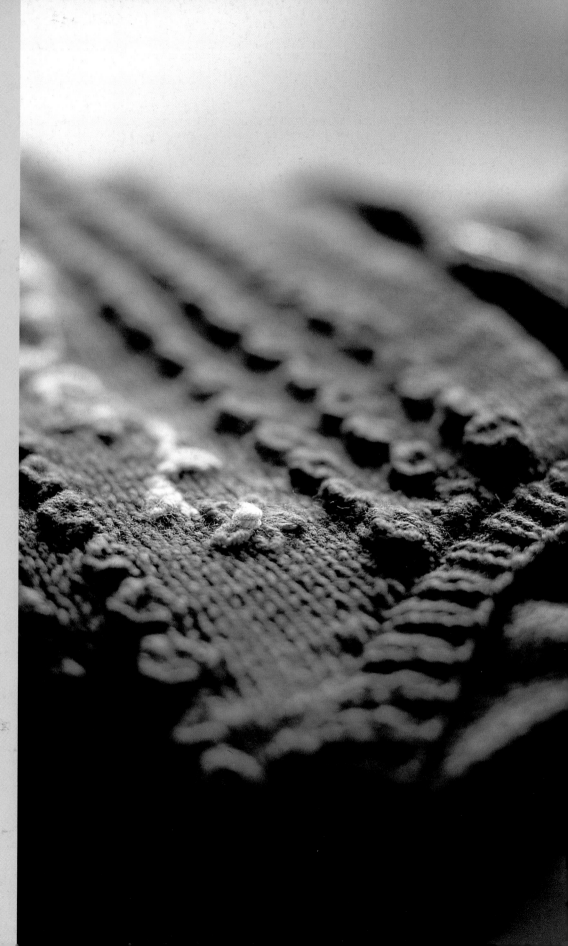

Tyrolean cardigan

SEE PATTERN ON PAGE 120

Women spent a great deal of time knitting a garment and were keen to display their skills and abilities, as exhibited in this contemporary translation of a Tyrolean cardigan.

Long-sleeved sweater with fairisle borders

SEE PATTERN ON PAGE 122

The borders of fairisle patterning on the body and sleeves of this sweater give a sporty touch to the garment. This is a good example of a design that requires a certain amount of knowledge and skill to make but is not too daunting for the novice knitter wishing to try out the technique of fairisle knitting.

Beaded sweater

SEE PATTERN ON PAGE 124

Evening sweaters are a very special item. The glittering sparkle of beads catching the light adds a touch of glamour to every girl's wardrobe.

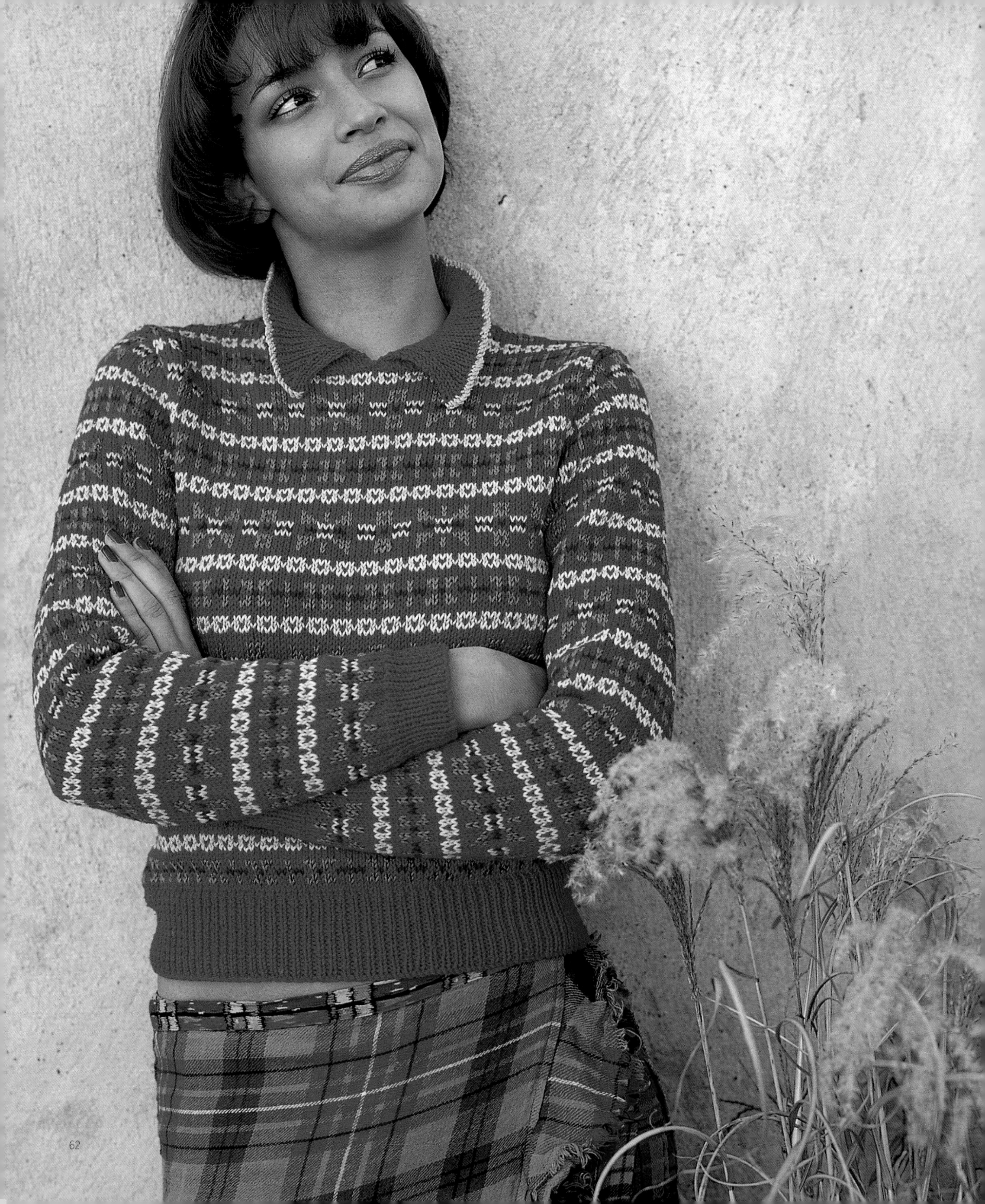

Long-sleeved fairisle sweater

SEE PATTERN ON PAGE 126

At this time there was a real wish to throw off the drabness and austerity of war. With the careful and considered use and placement of colours within the pattern of a fairisle sweater a vivacious mood could be created. This can be achieved even more so today with the abundant choice of colours and yarns now available.

Pattern information

Sizing

The sizes for the garments in this book are mainly small, medium and large, i.e. 81cm (32in), 86cm (34in) and 91cm (36in) chest measurement. As the inspiration for these designs originates from 1940s' and 1950s' knitting patterns, many of the garments are intentionally quite close fitting. However, some ease has been allowed, so check the final garment measurement before starting to knit.

The patterns quote both the chest measurement and the actual measurement of the finished, knitted garment.

Tension

Before knitting one of the designs in this book it is really important to check the tension of your knitting, to achieve accurate sizing, by knitting a tension swatch.

Each pattern states the yarn, needles and tension required. With this information, knit a sample square a little larger than 10cm (4in). Smooth out the finished sample on a flat surface and do not stretch it.

Using a ruler, measure out 10cm (4in) and count each stitch, including half stitches. Count the rows in the same manner. Check this against the tension required in the pattern instructions.

If you have too many stitches and rows, change to a larger size needle; if you have too few stitches and rows, change to a smaller needle and try another tension swatch.

Do check your tension carefully as one stitch or row wrongly calculated could lead to inaccurate sizing of the garment.

Yarns from different manufacturers may not knit to the tension in this book.

Yarn

Always try to use the yarn specified in the knitting instructions to achieve the best results. The yarn quantities given in the instructions are based on average requirements and should be considered approximate.

If you decide to substitute a yarn, if you cannot find the one recommended or you wish to use a different colour, be sure to choose a yarn as close as possible to the original, in fibre content, thickness, weight and meterage (yardage). Check the information on the ball band, and try a tension swatch to ensure it is compatible with the original yarn.

Washing instructions

Always check the washing and care instructions on the ball band of the yarn. Natural fibres such as wool, cotton and silk are generally better washed by hand using warm water and soap flakes. Make sure the soap flakes are completely dissolved before immersing the garment in the water. Rinse the garment thoroughly in clean cool water. Squeeze out the water but do not wring the garment. Roll the garment in a towel to squeeze out any excess water, or spin dry on a washing machine programme for delicate fabrics. Dry flat on a towel, away from direct heat, and ease the garment into shape. When the garment is dry, steam press gently with a damp cloth.

Sirdar

No. 1410
'MAJESTIC' 3-PLY
(Beaded Knitting)
Bust 34/35 inches
6ᴰ

Abbreviations

The following are the most commonly used abbreviations in the patterns. Some patterns have special abbreviations, which are given at the start of the relevant patterns.

Where cast off stitches are given in the middle of a row, the last stitch of the cast off is always included in the instructions that follow.

alt = alternate

beg = beginning

C = contrast colour

c4f = place next 2 sts on cable needle, leave at front of work, k2, k2 from cable needle

c4b = place next 2 sts on cable needle; leave at back of work, k2, k2 from cable needle

c6b = place next 3 sts on cable needle, leave at back of work, k3, k3 from cable needle

cont = continue

dec = decrease by knitting/purling the next 2 stitches together

foll(s) = follow(s)ing

inc = increase by knitting into the front and back of the next stitch

k = knit

k1b = knit next stitch through the back loop

k1, p1 rib = (on even number of sts) every row; k1, p1 to end

k1, p1 rib = (on odd number of sts) every RS row: *k1, p1* to last st, k1; every WS row: p1, *k1, p1* to end

M = main colour

m1 = make a stitch by picking up yarn before next stitch and knitting into the back of it

mp = make a stitch by picking up yarn before next stitch and purling into the back of it

p = purl

p1b = purl next stitch through the back loop

p2tog = purl next 2 stitches together

p2togb = purl next 2 stitches together through back of loops

p3tog = purl next 3 stitches together

patt = pattern

psso = pass slipped stitch over

rem = remain(ing)

rep = repeat

RS = right side

sl1(2) = slip next stitch (2 stitches) knitwise

sl1(3)p = slip next stitch (3 stitches) purlwise

st st = stocking stitch – row 1: knit, row 2: purl

st(s) = stitch(es)

tog = together

WS = wrong side

yb = yarn back

yf = yarn forward

yo = take yarn over or around needle to make a 'hole'

** = repeat enclosed instructions the number of times indicated

[] = repeat enclosed instructions the number of times indicated

() = brackets refer to larger size(s). Where only one figure is given it refers to all sizes.

Lace vest

PICTURED ON PAGE 8

SIZE

	Small	Medium	Large
to fit bust (cm)	76-81	84-89	91-94
to fit bust (in)	(30-32)	(33-35)	(36-37)
actual size	81 (32)	89 (35)	94 (37)
back length	30 (12)	30 (12)	30 (12)

MATERIALS

Rowan Cotton Glacé 50g balls:

candy floss (M)	4	5	5
bubbles (C)	1	1	1

1 pair each 2¾mm (US 2) and 3¼mm (US 3) needles

Spare needle

2m (2yd) of narrow ribbon

TENSION

24 sts and 28 rows = 10cm (4in) square over st st using Rowan cotton glacé and 3¼mm (US 3) needles.

ABBREVIATIONS

See page 67.

BACK

Using 2¾mm (US 2) needles and M, cast on 95(103:111) sts and work 7 rows in k1, p1 rib.

Change to 3¼mm (US 3) needles and work as folls:

Row 1 (WS): purl.

Row 2: k23(25:27), *yo, k2tog, k22(24:26); rep from * to end. **

Rep rows 1-2 until work measures 30cm (12in), ending with row 1. Leave sts on spare needle.

FRONT

Work as Back to **.

Rep rows 1-2 until work measures 18cm (7in), ending with row 1.

Cont as folls:

Row 1 (RS): k1, *yo, k2tog; rep from * to end.

Row 2: purl.

Row 3: k11(12:13), *yo, k2tog, k10(11:12); rep from * to end.

Row 4: purl.

Rep rows 3-4 until work measures 30cm (12in), ending with a WS row.

Shape armholes

Rows 1-2: cast off 4(5:6) sts, patt to end.

Rows 3-4: cast off 3(3:5) sts, patt to end.

Rows 5-6: cast off 2 sts, patt to end.

Row 7: patt 31(34:34), cast off 15(15:17) sts, patt to end.

Working on 31(34:34)sts:

Row 8: purl.

Row 9: k1, sl1, k1, psso, patt to end.

Row 10: purl.

Row 11: k1, sl1, k1, psso, patt to last 3 sts, k2tog, k1.

Row 12: purl.

Rows 13-16: as rows 9-12.

Sizes Medium and Large

Work rows 9-12 again. 25 sts.

All sizes

Row 17(21:21): as row 11.

Row 18(22:22): p1, p2tog, purl to last 3 sts, p2togb, p1.

Rep last 2 rows 4 times. 5 sts.

Row 27(31:31): k1, sl1, k2tog, psso, k1.

Row 28(32:32): p3tog. Fasten off.

Rejoin yarn to rem sts at centre front, purl to end (row 8).

Row 9: patt to last 3 sts, k2tog, k1.

Row 10: purl.

Row 11: k1, sl1, k1, psso, patt to last 3 sts, k2tog, k1.

Row 12: purl.

Rows 13-16: as rows 9-12.

Rows 17-28(32:32): as for first side.

TRIMS

Join side seams.

Side fronts and back

With RS facing and using 3¼mm (US 3) needles and M, pick up and knit 28(33:35) sts from point to side seam, knit across back sts, pick up and knit 28(33:35) sts from side seam to point. 151(169:181) sts.

Row 1: purl

Row 2: k3, *yo, k2tog, k4; rep from * to last 4 sts, yo, k2tog, k2.

Row 3: purl.

Row 4: change to 2¾mm (US 2) needles and C, cast off 3 sts, *slip st on right needle back onto left needle, cast on 2 sts, cast off 5 sts; rep from * to end. Fasten off.

Straps and centre front

Using 3¼mm (US 3) needles and M, cast on 69 sts. With RS facing, pick up and knit 4 sts from trim at front point, 16(19:21) sts from point to centre front, 15(15:17) sts from centre front, 16(19:21) sts from centre front to point, 4 sts from trim for side fronts and back, cast on 69 sts. 193(199:205) sts. Work as for side fronts and back trim.

FINISHING

Sew straps to back trim. Thread ribbon through trim eyelet holes (see photograph on page 8).

Cotton jacket with chenille edgings

PICTURED ON PAGE 10

SIZES

	Small	Medium	Large
to fit bust (cm)	81-86	88-91	94-96
to fit bust (in)	(32-34)	(35-36)	(37-38)
actual size	91 (36)	96 (38)	102 (40)
back length	53 (21)	53 (21)	53 (21)
sleeve seam	44 (17½)	44 (17½)	44 (17½)

MATERIALS

Rowan handknit dk cotton 50g balls:

gerba (M)	12	13	14

Rowan chunky chenille:

aubergine (C)	1	1	1

1 pair each 4½mm (US 7) and 4mm (US 6) needles

6 buttons

TENSION

20 sts and 28 rows = 10cm (4in) square over st st using Rowan handknit dk cotton and 4mm (US 6) needles.

ABBREVIATIONS

See page 67.

BACK

Using 4½mm (US 7) needles and C, cast on 75(81:87) sts. Change to 4mm (US 6) needles and work 5 rows in moss st (every row *k1, p1; rep from * to last st, k1).

Change to M and st st and work as folls:

Row 1: k2(3:4), [m1, k5] 14(15:16) times, m1, k3. 90(97:104) sts.

Row 2: purl.

Row 3: k2, k2tog, knit to last 4 sts, sl1, k1, psso, k2. Cont in st st, dec as set on rows 9, 15, 21 and 27. 80(87:94) sts.

Cont without shaping to completion of row 42.

Row 43: k2, m1, knit to last 2 sts, m1, k2. Inc as set each end of rows 49, 55, 61 and 67. 90(97:104) sts. Cont without shaping to completion of row 84.

Shape armholes

Rows 85-86: cast off 2(3:4) sts, work to end.

Rows 87-88: dec each end.

Dec each end of rows 89, 91 and 93. 76(81:86) sts. Cont to completion of row 140.

Shape shoulders and neck

Rows 141-142: cast off 6 sts, work to end.

Row 143: cast off 6 sts, k15(17:19), cast off 22(23:24) sts, work to end.

Working on 21(23:25)sts:

Row 144: cast off 6 sts, work to end.

Row 145: cast off 3 sts, work to end.

Row 146: cast off 5(6:7) sts, work to end.

Row 147: cast off 2 sts, work to end.

Row 148: cast off.

Rejoin yarn to rem sts at neck edge, work rows 145-148.

LEFT FRONT

**Using 4½mm (US 7) needles and C, cast on 42(45:48) sts. Change to 4mm (US 6) needles and work 5 rows in moss st, beg row 1 (WS), k1; end row 1, p1(k1:p1). Change to M and work as folls:

Row 1: k2(3:1), [m1, k4(4:5)] 8 times, m1, k2(4:1), *p1, k1; rep from * 3 times. ** 51(54:57) sts.

Row 2: *k1, p1; rep from * 3 times, purl to end.

Row 3: k2, k2tog, knit to last 6 sts, *p1, k1; rep from * 3 times.

Row 4: as row 2.

Keeping front border correct, dec as set beg rows 9, 15, 21 and 27. Cont to completion of row 42.

Row 43: k2, m1, knit to last 6 sts, *p1, k1; rep from * 3 times.

Keeping front border correct, inc as set beg rows 49, 55, 61 and 67. Cont to completion of row 84.

Shape armhole

Row 85: cast off 2(3:4) sts, patt to end.

Row 86: patt.

Rows 87-88: dec armhole edge, patt.

Dec armhole edge on rows 89, 91 and 93. 44(46:48) sts. Cont to completion of row 135.

Shape neck and shoulders

Row 136: cast off 10 sts, purl to end.

Row 137: knit.

Row 138: cast off 4 sts, purl to end.

Rows 139-140: as rows 137-138.

Row 141: cast off 6 sts, knit to last 2 sts, k2tog.

Row 142: dec, purl to end.

Rows 143-144: as rows 141-142.

Row 145: cast off 5(6:7) sts, knit to end.

Row 146: purl.

Row 147: cast off.

RIGHT FRONT

Using 4½mm (US 7) needles and C, cast on 42(45:48) sts. Change to 4mm (US 6) needles and work 5 rows in moss st, beg row 1 (WS): p1(k1:p1), end row 1, k1. Change to M and work as folls:

Row 1: *k1, p1; rep from * 3 times, k2(4:1), m1, [k4(4:5), m1] 8 times, k2(3:1). 51(54:57) sts.

Row 2: purl to last 5 sts, *k1, p1; rep from * twice, k1.

Row 3: *k1, p1; rep from * 3 times, knit to last 4 sts, sl1, k1, psso, k2.

Row 4: as row 2.

Keeping front border correct, dec as set at end of rows 9, 15, 21 and 27 and AT THE SAME TIME make buttonhole on rows 15-16 as folls:

Row 15: k1, p1, k1, cast off 1 st, k1, p1, knit to last 4 sts, sl1, k1, psso, k2.

Row 16: patt to last 3 sts, yo, k1, p1, k1.

Keeping front border correct, cont to completion of row 36.

Rows 37-38: make buttonhole in front border.

Rows 39-42: patt.

Row 43: patt to last 2 sts, m1, k2.

Keeping the front border correct, inc as set at end of rows 49, 55, 61 and 67 and AT THE SAME TIME make

buttonhole as before on rows 59-60. Cont to completion of row 85, making buttonhole on rows 81-82.

Shape armhole

Row 86: cast off 2(3:4) sts, patt to end.

Rows 87-135: work as Left Front.

Row 136: patt.

Shape neck and shoulders

Row 137: cast off 10 sts, knit to end.

Row 138: purl.

Row 139: cast off 4 sts, knit to end.

Row 140: purl.

Row 141: work as row 139.

Row 142: cast off 6 sts, purl to last 2 sts, p2tog.

Row 143: dec, knit to end.

Rows 144-145: work as rows 142-143.

Row 146: cast off 5(6:7) sts, purl to end.

Row 147: knit.

Row 148: cast off.

SLEEVES (make 2)

Using 4½mm (US 7) needles and C, cast on 39 sts. Change to 4mm (US 6) needles and work 5 rows in moss st. Change to M and st st and work as folls:

Row 1: *k2, m1, k2; rep from * 9 times, k2, m1, k1. 49 sts.

Row 2: purl.

Row 3: k2, m1, knit to last 2 sts, m1, k2.

Row 4: purl.

Cont in st st, inc as set every 10th (8th:8th) row to 73(75:77) sts. Cont without shaping until work measures 44cm (17½in), ending with a purl row.

Shape sleevehead

Cast off 2(3:4) sts beg next 2 rows.

Dec each end of next 2 rows.

Dec each end of alt rows to 35 sts.

Cast off 3 sts beg next 4 rows. Cast off.

COLLAR

Join shoulder seams.

With RS facing and using 4mm (US 6) needles and M, pick up and knit 29 sts from right front neck STARTING halfway across buttonhole band, 38(40:42) sts from back neck and 28 sts from left front, ENDING half way across buttonband. Work as folls:

Row 1: k1, p1, knit to last 2 sts, p1, k1.

Row 2: k1, p1, k1, purl to last 3 sts, k1, p1, k1.

Row 3: k1, p1, k1, m1, knit to last 3 sts, m1, k1, p1, k1.

Row 4: work as row 2.

Rows 5-20: work as rows 3-4 eight times.

Row 21: k1, p1, k1, m1, *k1, p1; rep from * to last 4 sts, k1, m1, k1, p1, k1.

Rows 22-24: *k1, p1; rep from * to last st, k1.

Row 25: cast off.

FINISHING

Join side seams and sleeve seams. Ease sleevehead into armhole, stitch. Weave in loose ends. Sew on buttons.

Short-sleeved fairisle sweater

PICTURED ON PAGE 12

SIZES

	Small	Medium	Large
to fit bust cm (in)	81 (32)	86 (34)	91 (36)
actual size	86 (34)	91 (36)	96 (38)
back length	51 (20)	52 (20½)	53 (21)
sleeve seam	12 (4¾)	12 (4¾)	12 (4¾)

MATERIALS

Rowan 4-ply Botany 50g balls:

| violet (M) | 3 | 4 | 4 |

For all sizes, Rowan 4-ply Botany 50g balls: 1 ball each, strawberry, fresh green and bay

Rowan fine cotton chenille: 1 ball each, crocus and catkin (C)

1 pair each 2¾mm (US 2) needles and 3¼mm (US 3) needles

TENSION

28 sts and 36 rows = 10cm (4in) square over st st using Rowan 4-ply Botany and 3¼mm (US 3) needles.

ABBREVIATIONS

See page 67.

BACK

Using 2¾mm (US 2) needles and C, cast on 117(127:137) sts.

Change to M and knit 1 row.

Work 27(27:33) rows in k1, p1 rib.

Change to 3¼mm (US 3) needles and st st and patt from chart, inc each end of 11th row and every foll 12th row to 127(135:141) sts working extra sts into patt.

Cont without shaping until work measures 31(31:32)cm (12(12:12½)in), ending with a WS row.

Shape armholes

Cast off 5(7:9) sts beg next 2 rows.

Dec each end of next 4 rows.

Dec each end of next and every foll alt row to 99(103:107) sts.

Cont without shaping until armhole measures 18(19:19)cm (7(7½:7½)in), ending with a WS row.

Shape shoulders and neck

Row 1: cast off 6 sts, patt 20(21:22) sts, cast off 47(49:51) sts, patt to end.

Row 2: cast off 6 sts, patt to end.

Row 3: patt.

Rows 4-7: work as rows 2-3 twice.

Row 8: cast off.

Rejoin yarns to rem sts at neck edge.

Work rows 3-8 again.

FRONT

Work as Back until armhole measures 14cm (5½in), ending with a WS row.

Shape neck

Patt 26(27:28), cast off 47(49:51) sts, patt to end.

On 26(27:28) sts cont in patt until armhole measures same as Back, ending at armhole edge.

Shape shoulders

Cast off 6 sts beg next and foll 2 alt rows.

Work 1 row. Cast off.

Rejoin yarn to rem sts at neck edge and work to match.

SLEEVES (make 2)

Using 2¾mm (US 2) needles and C, cast on 87(89:91) sts.

Change to M and knit 1 row.

Work 17 rows in k1, p1 rib.

Change to 3¼mm (US 3) needles and st st.

Work 2 rows.

Row 3: k2, inc, knit to last 4 sts, inc, k3.

Row 4: purl.

Rep rows 3-4 to 99(103:107) sts.

Cont without shaping until work measures 12cm (4¾in), ending with a WS row.

Shape sleevehead

Cast off 5(7:9) sts beg next 2 rows.

Dec each end of next 4 rows.

Row 5: k2, sl1, k1, psso, knit to last 4 sts, k2tog, k2.

Row 6: purl.

Rep rows 5-6 until 51 sts rem.

Dec each end of next 4 rows.

Cast off 4 sts beg next 4 rows. Cast off.

NECKBAND

Join right shoulder seam.

With RS facing and using 2¾mm (US 2) needles and M,

pick up and knit 22 sts down left side front neck, 1 st

from corner, 47(49:51) sts from centre front, 1 st from

corner, 22 sts up right front neck, 8 sts down side back

neck, 1 st from corner, 47(49:51) sts from centre back,

1 st from corner and 8 sts up side back neck.

Working in k1, p1 rib, cont as folls:

Row 1: rib 8, p1, rib 47(49:51), p1, rib 30, p1, rib

47(49:51), p1, rib 22.

Row 2: rib 20 *dec, k1, dec*, rib 43(45:47), rep from *

to *, rib 26, rep from * to *, rib 43(45:47), rep from * to

*, rib 6.

Row 3: rib 5, *dec, p1, dec*, rib 41(43:45), rep from *

to *, rib 24, rep from * to *, rib 41(43:45), rep from * to

*, rib 19.

Rows 4-5: dec as set.

Row 6: cast off in rib.

FINISHING

Join neckband and left shoulder seam. Weave in any

loose ends. Join side seams. Join sleeve seams. Ease

sleevehead into armhole and stitch into position.

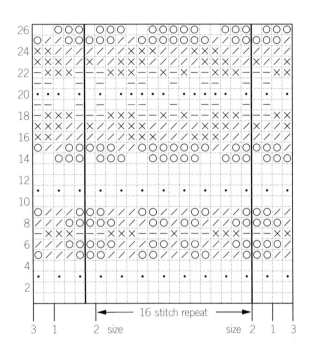

Key

☐ M, violet

☒ strawberry

⊙ bay

╱ fresh green

─ catkin

• crocus

Long-sleeved cotton jacket

PICTURED ON PAGE 14

SIZES

	Small	Medium	Large
to fit bust cm (in)	81 (32)	86 (34)	91 (36)
actual size	86 (34)	91 (36)	96 (38)
back length	54 (21¼)	54 (21¼)	56 (22¼)
sleeve seam	44 (17½)	44 (17½)	44 (17½)

MATERIALS

Rowan handknit dk cotton 50g balls:

lush	13	13	14

1 pair each 3¼mm (US 3) and 4mm (US 6) needles

9 buttons

Stitch holder

2 safety pins

TENSION

20 sts and 28 rows = 10cm (4in) square over st st using Rowan handknit dk cotton and 4mm (US 6) needles.

ABBREVIATIONS

See page 67.

BACK

Using 3¼mm (US 3) needles, cast on 85(91:97) sts and work 14 rows in k1, p1 rib.

Change to 4mm (US 6) needles and st st, inc each end of 13th and every foll 16th row to 91(97:103) sts.

Cont with shaping until work measures 32(32:33)cm (12½(12½:13)in), ending with a purl row.

Shape armholes

Rows 1-2: cast off 2(3:4) sts, work to end.

Row 3: k2, sl1, k1, psso, knit to last 4 sts, k2tog.

Row 4: purl.

Rep rows 3-4 until 77(81:83) sts rem.

Cont without shaping until work measures 51(51:53)cm (20(20:21)in), ending with a purl row.

Shape shoulders

Cast off 5 sts beg next 6 rows. Cast off 6(7:8) sts beg next 2 rows.

Cast off.

POCKETS (make 2)

Using 4mm (US 6) needles, cast on 18 sts and work 28 rows in st st. Leave on holder.

LEFT FRONT

Using 3¼mm (US 3) needles, cast on 46(49:52) sts and work 14 rows in k1, p1 rib.

Change to 4mm (US 6) needles and work as folls:

Row 1: k15(17:19), [p2, k2] 4 times, p2, k7(8:9) sts, leave 6 sts on safety pin for buttonband.

Row 2: purl.

Rows 1 and 2 form patt.

Cont in patt, inc beg of 13th and every foll 16th row to 43(46:49) sts.

Cont without shaping until work measures 32(32:33)cm (12½(12½:13)in), ending with a purl row.

Shape armhole

Row 1: cast off 2(3:4) sts, patt to end.

Row 2: purl.

Row 3: k2, sl1, k1, psso, patt to end.

Row 4: purl.

Rows 5-6: work as rows 3-4.

Row 7: k2, sl1, k1, psso, k10(11:12), [p2, k2] twice, cast off 2 sts, * k2, p2; rep from * twice, k7(8:9).

Row 8: p15(16:17), cast on 2 sts, purl to end.

Rows 9-10: work as rows 3-4.

Row 11: work as row 3.

Row 12: p7(8:9), cast off 18 sts, purl to end.

Row 13: k11(12:13), knit across pocket stitches, knit to end. 36(38:40) sts.

Row 14: purl.

Cont in st st, without shaping, until work measures 48(48:51)cm (19(19:20)in), ending with a knit row.

Shape neck

Cast off 6(7:8) sts, work to end.

Dec neck edge on next 6 rows, ending with a purl row.

Shape shoulder

Row 1: cast off 5 sts, work to last 2 sts, dec.

Row 2: work across sts.

Rows 3-6: work as rows 1-2 twice.

Row 7: cast off.

RIGHT FRONT

Using 3¼mm (US 3) needles, cast on 46(49:52) sts and work 2 rows in k1, p1 rib.

Row 3 (buttonhole row): rib 3, cast off 2 sts, rib to end.

Row 4: rib 41(44:47) sts, cast on 2 sts, rib 3.

Rows 5-12: rib.

Row 13: work as row 3.

Row 14: rib 40(43:46), place rem sts on safety pin. Change to 4mm (US 6) needles and patt as folls:

Row 1: k7(8:9), *p2, k2; rep from * 4 times, p2, k15(17:19).

Row 2: purl.

This sets patt panel.

Work to match Left Front, reversing all shapings.

SLEEVES (make 2)

Using 3¼mm (US 3) needles, cast on 46(48:50) sts and work 14 rows in k1, p1 rib.

Change to 4mm (US 6) needles and work as folls:

Row 1: k16(17:18), *p2, k2; rep from * 3 times, p2, k16(17:18).

Row 2: purl.

Rows 1 and 2 form patt panel.

Cont in patt, making fully fashioned incs by k2, inc, patt to last 4 sts, inc, k3, on 5th and every foll 6th row to 74(76:78) sts.

Cont without shaping until work measures 44cm (17½in).

Shape sleevehead

Cast off 2(3:4) sts beg next 2 rows.

Row 3: k2, sl1, k1, psso, patt to last 4 sts, k2tog, k2.

Row 4: purl.

Rep rows 3-4 until 46 sts rem.

Dec each end of next 4 rows.

Cast off 3 sts beg next 4 rows.

Cast off.

BUTTONBAND

With RS facing and using 3¼mm (US 3) needles, pick up thread between sts on safety pin and Left Front, knit into back of it, rib across sts on safety pin. 7 sts.

Cont in rib until band when slightly stretched fits front to neck shaping.

Cast off.

Stitch into place.

Mark positions for 5 buttonholes, approximately 8cm (3½in) apart, starting above rib and finishing 1cm (½in) below the neck.

BUTTONHOLE BAND

With WS facing and using 3¼mm (US 3) needles, pick up thread between sts on safety pin and Right Front,

knit into back of it, rib 1, cast on 2 sts, rib 3. 7sts.

Cont in rib making 5 further buttonholes, to match marked positions, as folls:

Row 1: rib 3, cast off 2 sts, rib 2.

Row 2: rib 2, cast on 2 sts, rib 3.

Work to match buttonband length.

Cast off.

Stitch into place.

COLLAR

Using 4mm (US 6) needles, cast on 90(90:94) sts and work as folls:

Row 1: *p2, k2; rep from * to last 2 sts, p2.

Row 2: purl.

Rep rows 1-2 until work measures 8cm (3in) ending with row 1.

Next row: p2(2:4), *p2tog, p4; rep from * to last 4(4:6) sts, p2tog, p2(2:4).

Cast off.

FINISHING

Slipstitch pockets into position. Join shoulder and side seams. Join sleeve seams. Ease sleevehead into armhole and stitch into place. Place RS of collar to WS of garment, cast off collar edge to neck, starting and finishing halfway across front bands. Oversew into place. Weave in any loose ends. Sew buttons on buttonband and to match buttonholes on pockets.

Short-sleeved diamond stitch sweater

PICTURED ON PAGE 16

SIZES

	Small	Medium
to fit bust (cm)	81-84	86-91
to fit bust (in)	(32-33)	(34-36)
actual size	88 (34½)	98 (38½)
back length	51 (20)	51 (20)
sleeve seam	12 (4¾)	12 (4¾)

MATERIALS

Jaeger Matchmaker 4-ply 50g balls:

crush (M)	4	5
Rowan Kidsilk Haze 25g balls:		
poison (C)	1	1

1 pair each 2¾mm (US 2) and 3¼mm (US 3) needles

Stitch holder

TENSION

30 sts and 40 rows = 10cm (4in) square over patt using Jaeger Matchmaker 4-ply and 3¼mm (US 3) needles.

ABBREVIATIONS

See page 67.

BACK

Using 2¾mm (US 2) needles and two ends of C, cast on 117(131) sts. Change to M and knit 1 row.

Work 7cm (2½in) rows in k1, p1 rib.

Change to 3¼mm (US 3) needles and patt as folls:

Row 1 (RS): k2, *p1, k13; rep from * 8(9) times, p1, k2.

Row 2: *p1, k1; rep from * twice, *p11, k1, p1, k1; rep from * 8(9) times, p1.

Row 3: *p1, k3, p1, k9; rep from * 8(9) times, p1, k3, p1.

Row 4: *p5, k1, p7, k1; rep from * 8(9) times, p5.

Row 5: k6, *p1, k5, p1, k7; rep from * 7(8) times, p1, k5, p1, k6.

Row 6: p7, *k1, p3, k1, p9; rep from * 7(8) times, k1, p3, k1, p7.

Row 7: k8, *p1, k1, p1, k11; rep from * 7(8) times, p1, k1, p1, k8.

Row 8: p9, *k1, p13; rep from * 7(8) times, k1, p9.

Row 9: as row 7.

Row 10: as row 6.

Row 11: as row 5.

Row 12: as row 4.

Row 13: as row 3.

Row 14: as row 2.

Rows 1-14 form patt rep.

Cont in patt, inc each end of next and every foll 8th row to 133(147) sts, working extra sts into patt.

Cont without shaping until work measures 31cm (12¼in), ending with a WS row.

Shape armholes

Cast off 5(8) sts beg next 2 rows.

Dec at each end of next 4 rows.

Dec each end of next and every foll alt row to 103(109) sts.

Cont without shaping until armhole measures 49cm (19¼in), ending with a WS row. Note pattern row.

Shape shoulders and neck

Cast off 5(6) sts beg next 4 rows.

Row 5: cast off 5 sts, patt 16 sts, cast off 41(43) sts, patt to end.

Row 6: cast off 5 sts, patt to end.

Row 7: cast off 3 sts, patt to end.

Row 8: cast off 5 sts, patt to end.

Row 9: cast off 2 sts, patt to end.

Row 10: cast off.

Rejoin yarn to rem sts at neck edge.

Work rows 7-10 again.

FRONT

Work as Back until Front is 18 rows less than Back to shoulder shaping, i.e. 1 complete patt and 4 rows.

Shape neck

Row 1: patt 39(41), turn.

Working on these 39(41) sts:

Rows 2-8: dec neck edge, patt.

Rows 9-18: dec neck edge on alt rows. 27(29) sts.

Shape shoulder

Row 19: cast off 5(6) sts, patt to last 2 sts, dec.

Row 20: patt.

Row 21: cast off 5(6) sts, patt to end.

Row 22: patt.

Row 23: cast off 5 sts, patt to end.

Row 24: patt.

Rows 25-26: as rows 23-24.

Row 27: cast off.

Slip 25(27) sts onto st holder.

Rejoin yarn to rem sts at neck edge,

work to match first side.

SLEEVES (make 2)

Using 2¾mm (US 2) needles and two ends of C, cast
on 87 sts.

Change to M and knit 1 row.

Work 4cm (1¾in) in k1, p1 rib.

Change to 3¼mm (US 3) needles and patt as folls:

Row 1: k1, *p1, k13; rep from * 6 times, p1, k1.

This sets patt as on Back.

Cont in patt, inc each end of 3rd and every foll 4th (3rd)
row to 99(103) sts, working extra sts into patt.

Cont without shaping until work measures 12cm (4¾in).

Shape sleevehead

Cast off 5(8) sts beg next 2 rows.

Dec each end of next 4 rows.

Dec each end of next and every foll alt row to 51 sts.

Dec each end of next 6 rows.

Cast off 3 sts beg next 4 rows.

Cast off.

NECKBAND

Join right shoulder seam.

With RS facing and using 2¾mm (US 2) needles and M,

pick up and knit 24 sts down left side front neck,

25(27) sts from holder, 24 sts up right side neck and

55(57) sts from back neck.

Work 2cm (¾in) k1, p1 rib.

Cast off loosely in rib.

FINISHING

Join left shoulder seam and neckband. Join side seams
and sleeve seams. Ease sleevehead into armhole and
stitch into place. Weave in any loose ends.

Cable sweater

PICTURED ON PAGE 18

SIZES

	Small	Medium	Large
to fit bust (cm)	81-86	88-91	94-96
to fit bust (in)	(32-34)	(35-36)	(37-38)
actual size	91 (36)	96 (38)	102 (40)
back length	56 (22)	56 (22)	56 (22)
sleeve seam	46 (18)	46 (18)	46 (18)

MATERIALS

Rowan handknit dk cotton 50g balls:

lupin	12	13	14

1 pair each 3¼mm (US 3) and 4mm (US 6) needles

Stitch holders

Cable needle

TENSION

20 sts and 28 rows = 10cm (4in) square over st st using Rowan handknit dk cotton and 4mm (US 6) needles.

ABBREVIATIONS

See page 67.

BACK

Using 3¼mm (US 3) needles, cast on 87(91:97) sts and work 8cm (3in) in k1, p1 rib.

Change to 4mm (US 6) needles and st st, inc each end of 13th and every foll 16th row to 93(97:103) sts.

Cont without shaping until work measures 34cm (13½in), ending with a WS row.

Shape armholes

Rows 1-2: cast off 2(3:4) sts, work to end.

Rows 3-4: dec each end.

Row 5: k2, sl1, k1, psso, knit to last 4 sts, k2tog, k2.

Row 6: purl.

Dec as row 5, each end of next and every foll alt row to 79(81:83) sts.

Cont without shaping until work measures 53cm (21in), ending with a WS row. ***

Shape shoulders

Cast off 6 sts beg next 6 rows.

Cast off 4(5:6) sts beg next 2 rows.

Leave rem sts on holder.

FRONT

Work as Back to ***.

Shape shoulders and neck

Row 1: cast off 6 sts, k26(27:28), turn.

Row 2: cast off 4 sts, purl to end.

Row 3: cast off 6 sts, knit to end.

Row 4: cast off 3 sts, purl to end.

Row 5: cast off 6 sts, knit to end.

Row 6: cast off 3 sts, purl to end.

Row 7: cast off.

Place 15 sts on holder.

Rejoin yarn to rem sts at neck edge, knit to end.

Work to match first shoulder.

SLEEVES (make 2)

Using 3¼mm (US 3) needles, cast on 48(50:52) sts and work 6cm (2½in) in k1, p1 rib.

Inc row: rib 23(24:25), m1, rib 2, m1, rib to end.

Change to 4mm (US 6) needles and work as folls:

Row 1: k20(21:22), p2, k6, p2, k20(21:22).

Row 2: p20(21:22), k2, p6, k2, p20(21:22).

Rows 3-4: as rows 1-2.

Row 5: k2, inc, k17(18:19), p2, c6b, p2, k17(18:19), inc, k2.

Row 6: p21(22:23), k2, p6, k2, p21(22:23).

Rows 1-6 form cable rep.

Cont in patt, inc as set on every foll 8th row to 74(74:76) sts.

Cont without shaping until work measures 46cm (18in), ending with a WS row.

Shape sleevehead

Cast off 2(3:4) sts beg next 2 rows.

Dec each end of next 2 rows.

Next row: k2, sl1, k1, psso, patt to last 4 sts, k2tog, k2.

Dec as set on every foll alt row to 30 sts.

Dec each end of next 4 rows.

Cast off 3 sts beg next 4 rows. 10 sts.

Work 12(12:13)cm (4¾:(4¾ :5)in) in cable patt.

Cast off.

FINISHING

Carefully pin cable extension of one Sleeve across right
shoulder shapings, back and front. Stitch into place. Ease
sleevehead into armhole and stitch. Pin cable extension
of the other Sleeve to Front only and stitch. Ease
sleevehead into Front armhole and stitch.

NECKBAND

With RS facing and using 3¼mm (US 3) needles, pick
up and knit 7 sts across cable, 14 sts down front neck,
15 sts from holder, 14 sts up front neck, 7 sts across
cable and 35 sts from holder.

Work 5cm (2in) in k1, p1 rib.

Cast off.

COMPLETE FINISHING

Join neckband, last shoulder seam and remaiming part
sleevehead. Join side and sleeve seams. Weave in any
loose ends.

Ribbed sweater

PICTURED ON PAGE 20

SIZES

	Small	Medium	Large
to fit bust cm (in)	81 (32)	86 (34)	91 (36)
actual size	86 (34)	91 (36)	96 (38)
back length	51 (20)	51 (20)	54 (21¼)
sleeve seam	46 (18)	46 (18)	46 (18)

MATERIALS

Rowan Cotton Glacé 50g balls:

hyacinth	9	9	10

1 pair each 3mm (US 2) and 3¼mm (US 3) needles

Stitch holders

TENSION

28 sts and 28 rows = 10cm (4in) square over k2, p2 rib using Rowan Cotton Glacé and 3¼mm (US 3) needles.

ABBREVIATIONS

See page 67.

BACK

Using 3mm (US 2) needles, cast on 106(114:122) sts and work 7cm (2¾in) in k2, p2 rib.

Change to 3¼mm (US 3) needles and cont in rib, inc each end of 5th and every foll 8th row to 118(126:134) sts, working extra sts into patt.

Cont without shaping until work measures 29(29:32)cm (11½(11½:12½)in), ending with a WS row.

Shape armholes

Cast off 4(5:6) sts beg next 2 rows.

Dec each end next 4 rows.

Dec each end of next and every foll alt row to 96(100:104) sts.

Cont without shaping until work measures 48(48:51)cm (19(19:20)in), ending with a WS row.

Shape shoulders and neck

Row 1: cast off 6(7:8) sts, patt 26, turn.

Working on these 26 sts:

Row 2: cast off 2 sts, patt to end.

Row 3: cast off 6 sts, patt to end.

Row 4: as row 2.

Row 5: cast off 7 sts, patt to end.

Row 6: as row 2.

Row 7: cast off.

Place centre 32(34:36) sts on holder.

Rejoin yarn to neck edge, patt to end.

Work rows 1-7 again.

FRONT

Work as Back until Front measures 42(42:44)cm (16½(16½:17¼)in), ending with a WS row.

Shape neck: patt 38(39:40) sts, turn.

Working on these 38(39:40) sts, dec neck edge on next 12 rows. 26(27:28) sts.

Cont without shaping until work measures same as Back at shoulder, ending with a WS row.

Shape shoulder

Row 1: cast off 6(7:8) sts, patt to end.

Row 2: patt.

Row 3: cast off 6 sts, patt to end.

Row 4: patt.

Row 5: cast off 7 sts, patt to end.

Row 6: patt.

Row 7: cast off.

Place centre 20(22:24) sts on holder.

Rejoin yarn to rem sts at neck edge, patt to end.

Work rows 1-7 again.

SLEEVES (make 2)

Using 3mm (US 2) needles, cast on 56(58:60) sts and work 5cm (2in) in k2, p2 rib.

Change to 3¼mm (US 3) needles and cont in rib.

Inc each end of 3rd and every foll 6th row to 84(88:92) sts, working extra sts into patt.

Cont without shaping until work measures 46cm (18in).

Shape sleevehead

Cast off 4(5:6) sts beg next 2 rows.

Dec each end of next 4 rows.

Dec each end of next and every foll alt row to
38(40:42) sts.

Dec each end of next 6 rows.

Cast off 4 sts beg next 4 rows.

Cast off.

NECKBAND

Join right shoulder seam.

With RS facing and using 3mm (US 2) needles, pick up
and knit 24 sts down side front neck, 20(22:24) sts
from holder, 24 sts up side front neck, 8 sts from side
back neck, 32(34:36) sts from holder and 8 sts from
side back neck.

Work 7 rows in k2, p2 rib.

Cast off.

FINISHING

Join neckband and left shoulder seam. Join side seams
and sleeve seams. Ease sleevehead into armhole and
stitch into place. Weave in any loose ends.

Short-sleeved cardigan with bow

PICTURED ON PAGE 22

SIZES

	Small	Medium	Large
to fit bust cm (in)	81 (32)	86 (34)	91 (36)
actual size	86 (34)	91 (36)	96 (38)
back length	50 (19¾)	50 (19¾)	50 (19¾)
sleeve seam	13 (5)	13 (5)	13 (5)

MATERIALS

Rowan Cotton Glacé 50g balls:

candy floss (M)	8	8	9
hyacinth (C)	1	1	1

1 pair each 2¾mm (US 2) and 4mm (US 6) needles

7 buttons

TENSION

24 sts and 30 rows = 10cm (4in) square over patt using Rowan Cotton Glacé and 4mm (US 6) needles.

ABBREVIATIONS

See page 67.

X2 = k the 2nd st on left needle and take st off over the 1st st, then k the 1st st

BACK

Using 2¾mm (US 2) needles and C, cast on 91(99:107) sts.

Change to M and work 8cm (3in) in k1, p1 rib, ending with a RS row.

Change to 4mm (US 6) needles and purl 1 row. Work patt as folls:

Row 1: k1, *X2, k2; rep from * to last 2 sts, X2.

Row 2: purl.

Row 3: k3, *X2, k2; rep from * to end.

Row 4: purl.

These 4 rows form patt rep.

Cont in patt, inc each end of 11th and every foll 10th row to 101(109:117) sts, working extra sts into patt.

Cont without shaping until work measures 29cm (11½in), ending with a WS row.

Shape armholes

Cast off 3(4:5) sts beg next 2 rows.

Dec each end next 4 rows.

Dec each end of next and every foll alt row to 81(87:93) sts. Cont without shaping until work measures 48cm (19in), ending with a WS row.

Shape shoulders and neck

Rows 1-2: cast off 5(6:6) sts, patt to end.

Row 3: cast off 5(6:6) sts, patt 16(16:17), cast off 29(31:35) sts, patt to end.

Row 4: cast off 5(6:6) sts, patt to end.

Row 5: cast off 3 sts, patt to end.

Row 6: cast off 6 sts, patt to end.

Row 7: cast off 2 sts, patt to end.

Row 8: cast off.

Rejoin yarn to rem sts at neck edge and work rows 5-8 again.

LEFT FRONT

Using 2¾mm (US 2) needles and C, cast on 43(47:51) sts.

Change to M and work 8cm (3in) in k1, p1 rib, ending with a RS row.

Change to 4mm (US 6) needles and purl 1 row.

Cont in patt as on Back, inc beg of 11th and every foll 10th row to 48(52:56) sts.

Cont without shaping until work measures 29cm (11½in), ending with a WS row.

Shape armhole

Cast off 3(4:5) sts, work to end.

Dec armhole edge on next 4 rows.

Dec armhole edge on next and every foll alt row to 38(41:44) sts.

Cont without shaping until work is 13 rows less than Back to shoulder, ending with a knit row.

Shape neck

Cast off 7(8:10) sts, patt to end.

Dec neck edge on next 2 rows.

Dec neck edge on next and every foll alt row to 24(26:27) sts, ending with a purl row.

Shape shoulder

Row 1: cast off 5(6:6) sts, patt to last 2 sts, k2tog.

Row 2: purl.

Rows 3-4: work as rows 1-2.

Row 5: cast off 6 sts, patt to last 2 sts, k2tog.

Row 6: purl.

Row 7: cast off.

RIGHT FRONT

Work as for Left Front, reversing all shapings.

SLEEVES

Using 2¾mm (US 2) needles and C, cast on 71(75:75) sts.

Change to M and work 4cm (1½in) in k1, p1 rib, ending with a RS row.

Change to 4mm (US 6) needles and purl 1 row.

Change to patt as on Back, inc each end of 3rd and every foll 3rd row to 85(87:91) sts, working extra sts into patt.

Cont without shaping until work measures 13cm (5in), ending with a WS row.

Shape sleevehead

Cast off 3(4:5) sts beg next 2 rows.

Dec each end next 4 rows.

Dec each end of next and every foll alt row to 41 sts.

Dec each end of next 4 rows.

Cast off 3 sts beg next 4 rows.

Cast off.

BUTTONBAND

Using 2¾mm (US 2) needles and M, cast on 7 sts.

Work in k1, p1 rib until band, when slightly stretched, reaches from hem to neck.

Cast off.

Mark positions for buttons: the 1st 1cm (½in) from hem, the 2nd level with top of welt rib, the 7th 4cm (1½in) down from the neck and the 3rd to 6th evenly spaced between the 2nd and 7th.

BUTTONHOLE BAND

Using 2¾mm (US 2) needles and M, cast on 7 sts.

Work to match buttonband making buttonholes to correspond with marked button positions by:

Row 1: rib 3, cast off 1 st, rib to end.

Row 2: rib 3, yo, rib 3.

NECK TRIM

Using 2¾mm (US 2) needles and M, cast on 7 sts.

Work 76cm (30in) in k1, p1 rib.

Cast off.

FINISHING

Join shoulder seams. Join side and sleeve seams. Ease sleevehead into armhole and stitch into position. Attach front bands. Attach neck trim, placing centre of neck trim to centre back neck. Stitch to halfway across front bands so ends of trim are free to tie into a bow. Weave in any loose ends. Sew on buttons.

Short-sleeved ribbed lace sweater

PICTURED ON PAGE 24

SIZES

	Small	Medium	Large
to fit bust cm (in)	81 (32)	86 (34)	91 (36)
actual size	86 (34)	91 (36)	96 (38)
back length	48 (18¾)	48 (18¾)	50 (19¾)
sleeve seam	11 (4¼)	11 (4¼)	11 (4¼)

MATERIALS

Rowan linen drape 50g balls:

petal	8	8	9

1 pair each 2¾mm (US 2) and 3¼mm (US 3) needles

Stitch holder

TENSION

28 sts and 30 rows = 10cm (4in) square over patt when blocked, using Rowan linen drape and 3¼mm (US 3) needles.

ABBREVIATIONS

See page 67.

BACK

Using 2¾mm (US 2) needles, cast on 108(116:124) sts and work in k2, p2 rib as folls:

Row 1: k1, *p2, k2; rep from * to last 3 sts, p2, k1.

Row 2: p1, *k2, p2; rep from * to last 3 sts, k2, p1.

Rep rows 1 and 2 until work measures 7cm (2¾in) ending with row 2.

Change to 3¼mm (US 3) needles and patt as folls:

Row 1 (RS): k1, *p2, yo, sl1, k1, psso, p2, k2; rep from * to last 3 sts, p2, k1.

Row 2: p1, *k2, p2; rep from * to last 3 sts, k2, p1.

Row 3: k1, *p2, k2tog, yo, p2, k2; rep from * to last 3 sts, p2, k1.

Row 4: as row 2.

Rows 5-8: as rows 1-4.

Row 9: k1, *p2, k2, p2, yo, sl1, k1, psso; rep from * to last 3 sts, p2, k1.

Row 10: as row 2.

Row 11: k1, *p2, k2, p2, k2tog, yo; rep from * to last 3 sts, p2, k1.

Row 12: as row 2.

Rows 13-16: as rows 9-12.

These 16 rows form patt rep.

Cont in patt, inc each end of next and every foll 10th row to 116(124:132) sts, working extra sts into patt.

Cont without shaping until work measures 27(27:29)cm (10½(10½:11½)in), ending with a WS row.

Shape armholes

Cast off 3(4:5) sts beg next 2 rows.

Dec at each end of next 4 rows.

Dec each end of next and every foll alt row to 92(96:100) sts.

Cont without shaping until work measures 46(46:48)cm (18(18:19)in), ending with a WS row.

Shape shoulders and neck

Cast off 6 sts beg next 2 rows.

Row 3: cast off 6 sts, patt 17(19:21) sts, cast off 34 sts, patt to end.

Row 4: cast off 6 sts, patt to end.

Row 5: cast off 3 sts, patt to end.

Row 6: cast off 6 sts, patt to end.

Row 7: cast off 2 sts, patt to end.

Row 8: cast off.

Rejoin yarn to rem sts at neck edge.

Work rows 5-8 again.

FRONT

Work as Back until Front is 16 rows less than Back to shoulder shaping, ending with WS row.

Shape neck

Row 1: patt 36(38:40) sts, turn.

Rows 2-13: dec neck edge.

Rows 14-16: patt.

Shape shoulder

Row 1: cast off 6 sts, patt to end.

Row 2: patt.

Rows 3-4: as rows 1-2.

Row 5: cast off 6 sts, patt to end.

Row 6: patt.

Row 7: cast off.

Place 20 sts on holder.

Rejoin yarn to rem sts at neck edge, patt to end.

Work to match first side.

SLEEVES (make 2)

Using 2¾mm (US 2) needles, cast on 76(84:84) sts and
work 5cm (2in) in k2, p2 rib as on Back.

Change to 3¼mm (US 3) needles and patt as on Back.

Inc each end of 3rd and every foll 3rd row to
86(90:94) sts.

Cont without shaping until work measures 11cm (4¼in).

Shape sleevehead

Cast off 4(5:6) sts beg next 2 rows.

Dec each end of next 4 rows.

Dec each end of next and every foll alt row to 40 sts.

Dec each end of next 6 rows.

Cast off 3 sts beg next 4 rows.

Cast off.

NECKBAND

Join right shoulder seam.

With RS facing and using 2¾mm (US 2) needles, pick
up and knit 22 sts down front side neck, 20 sts from
holder, 23 sts up side front neck and 45 sts
from back neck.

Work 6 rows in k2, p2 rib.

Cast off loosely in rib.

FINISHING

Join left shoulder seam and neckband. Join side and
sleeve seams. Ease sleevehead into armhole and stitch
into place. Weave in any loose ends.

Long-sleeved ribbed cardigan

PICTURED ON PAGE 26

SIZES

	Small	Medium	Large
to fit bust cm (in)	81 (32)	86 (34)	91 (36)
actual size	86 (34)	91 (36)	96 (38)
back length	53 (21)	53 (21)	53 (21)
sleeve seam	46 (18)	46 (18)	46 (18)

MATERIALS

Rowan linen drape 50g balls:

hawaii	11	11	12

1 pair each 3mm (US 2) and 3¼mm (US 3) needles

2 stitch holders

7 buttons

TENSION

28 sts and 28 rows = 10cm (4in) square over k2, p2 rib using Rowan linen drape and 3¼mm (US 3) needles.

ABBREVIATIONS

See page 67.

BACK

Using 3mm (US 2) needles, cast on 106(114:122) sts and work 7cm (2¾in) in k2, p2 rib (row 1 (RS): *k2, p2; rep from * to last 2 sts, k2), ending with a WS row. Change to 3¼mm (US 3) needles and cont in rib, inc each end of 5th and every foll 8th row to 118(126:134) sts, working extra sts into patt.

Cont without shaping until work measures 29cm (11½in), ending with a WS row.

Shape armholes

Cast off 4(5:6) sts beg next 2 rows.

Dec each end next 4 rows.

Dec each end of next and every foll alt row to 90(96:102) sts.

Cont without shaping until work measures 51cm (20in), ending with a WS row.

Shape shoulders

Cast off 5(6:7) sts beg next 2 rows.

Row 3: cast off 5(6:7) sts, patt 19, cast off 32(34:36) sts, patt to end.

Row 4: cast off 5(6:7) sts, patt to end.

Row 5: cast off 3 sts, patt to end.

Row 6: cast off 6 sts, patt to end.

Row 7: cast off 3 sts, patt to end.

Row 8: cast off.

Rejoin yarn to rem sts at neck edge and work rows 5-8 again.

LEFT FRONT

Using 3mm (US 2) needles, cast on 58(62:66) sts and work 7cm (2¾in) in k2, p2 rib as on Back, ending with a WS row.

Change to 3¼mm (US 3) needles and cont in rib, inc beg of 5th and every foll 8th row to 64(68:72) sts.

Cont without shaping until work measures 29cm (11½in), ending with a WS row.

Shape armhole

Cast off 4(5:6) sts, patt to end.

Work 1 row.

Dec armhole edge on next 4 rows.

Dec armhole edge on next and every foll alt row to 50(53:56) sts.

Cont without shaping until work measures 46cm (18in), ending with a WS row.

**Shape neck

Patt 34(36:38) sts, place 16(17:18) sts on holder for neckband.

Dec neck edge on every row to 23(25:27) sts.

Cont without shaping to match Back length at shoulder, ending with a WS row.

Shape shoulder

Row 1: cast off 5(6:7) sts, patt to end.

Row 2: patt.

Rows 3-4: work as rows 1-2.

Row 5: cast off 6 sts, patt to end.

Row 6: patt.

Row 7: cast off.

RIGHT FRONT

Using 3mm (US 2) needles, cast on 58(62:66) sts and work 4 rows in k2, p2 rib.

Buttonhole rows

Row 5: k2, p2, cast off 2 sts, patt to end.

Row 6: Patt 52(56:60), cast on 2 sts, k2, p2.

Cont in rib until work measures 2 rows less than Left Front welt rib.

Make 2nd buttonhole as rows 5 and 6.

Change to 3¼mm (US 3) needles and cont in rib, inc end of 5th row and every foll 8th row to 64(68:72) sts and AT THE SAME TIME make further buttonholes at 15cm (6in) and 23cm (9in).

Cont without shaping until work measures 29cm (11½in), ending with a RS row.

Shape armhole

Cast off 4(5:6) sts, patt to end.

Dec armhole edge on next 4 rows.

Dec armhole edge on next and every foll alt row to 50(53:56) sts and AT THE SAME TIME make 5th buttonhole at 31cm (12¼in).

Cont without shaping until work measures 46cm (18in), making 6th buttonhole at 39cm (15¼in), and ending with a RS row.

Work from ** to end of Left Front reversing shapings.

SLEEVES (make 2)

Using 3mm (US 2) needles, cast on 54(58:62) sts and work 5cm (2in) in k2, p2 rib, ending with a WS row. Change to 3¼mm (US 3) needles and cont in rib. Inc each end of 3rd row and every foll 6th row to 84(88:92) sts, working extra sts into patt. Cont without shaping until work measures 46cm (18in), ending with a WS row.

Shape sleevehead

Cast off 4(5:6) sts beg next 2 rows.

Dec each end of next 4 rows.

Dec each end of next and every foll alt row to 58(60:62) sts.

Cont without shaping until sleevehead measures 11cm (4¼in), ending with a WS row.

Work darts

Next row: patt 38(39:40) sts, turn, patt 18, turn.

On these 18 sts, work 5cm (2in) in rib. Cast off.

Rejoin yarn to first set of 20(21:22) sts at centre of sleeve.

Row 1: cast off 2 sts, patt to last 2 sts, dec.

Row 2: patt to last 2 sts, dec.

Rep rows 1 and 2 until 4(5:6) sts rem.

Cast off.

Rejoin yarn to rem sts at centre and work to match.

NECKBAND

Join shoulder seams.

With RS facing and using 3mm (US 2) needles, knit across 16(17:18) sts on holder, pick up and knit 21 sts from side edge front neck, 44(46:48) sts from back neck, 21 sts down left front and 16(17:18) sts from holder.

Beg with a WS row, work 3 rows in k2, p2 rib.

Rows 4 and 5: make buttonhole as Right Front.

Work 2 more rows in rib.

Cast off in rib.

FINISHING

Join side seams. Join sleeve darts, leaving final 4(5:6) cast off sts to be part of sleevehead. Join sleeve seams. Ease sleevehead into armhole and stitch into place. Sew on buttons. Weave in any loose ends.

Short-sleeved sweater with mohair stripe

PICTURED ON PAGE 28

SIZES

	Small	Medium	Large
to fit bust cm (in)	81 (32)	86 (34)	91 (36)
actual size	86 (34)	91 (36)	96 (38)
back length	50 (19¾)	50 (19¾)	50 (19¾)
sleeve seam	12 (4¾)	12 (4¾)	12 (4¾)

MATERIALS

Rowan 4-ply Botany 50g balls:

viola (M)	5	5	6

Rowan Kidsilk Haze 25g balls:

jelly (C)	2	2	2

1 pair 2¾mm (US 2) needles and a 3¼mm (US 3)
circular needle

Stitch holder

TENSION

28 sts and 36 rows = 10cm (4in) square over st st using
Rowan 4-ply Botany and 3¼mm (US 3) needles.

ABBREVIATIONS

See page 67.

NOTE

When working odd row striped patts, a circular needle
helps avoid lots of ends. Work first 10-row rep. The M
yarn is at the 'wrong end' for normal knitting, so turn
work to WS facing and start second rep with a purl row
taking the C yarn up the side of the knitting where it will
be in the correct position for use later. Turn the work
again and start third rep with a knit row, etc.

BACK

Using 2¾mm (US 2) needles and M, cast on
109(117:125) sts and work 6cm (2½in) in k1, p1 rib.
Change to 3¼mm (US 3) circular needle and st st and
work stripe patt of 9 rows M, 1 row C (using two ends
of C).

Inc each end of 7th row and every foll 8th row to
119(127:135) sts.

Cont to completion of row 84, ending with a purl row.

Shape armholes

Cast off 4(5:6) sts beg next 2 rows.

Dec at each end of next 4 rows.

Dec each end of next and every foll alt row to
91(97:103) sts.

Cont without shaping to completion of row 150, ending
with a purl row. Break C.

Shape shoulders and neck

Cast off 5 sts beg next 2 rows.

Row 3: cast off 5 sts, patt 15(18:20) sts, cast off
41(41:43) sts, patt to end.

Row 4: cast off 5 sts, patt to end.

Row 5: cast off 3 sts, patt to end.

Row 6: cast off 5(6:7) sts, patt to end.

Row 7: cast off 2 sts, patt to end.

Row 8: cast off.

Rejoin yarn to rem sts at neck edge.

Work rows 5-8 inclusive.

FRONT

Work as Back to completion of row 134, ending with a knit row.

Row 135: patt 31(34:36), turn.

Working on these 31(34:36) sts:

Rows 136-142: dec neck edge.

Rows 143-150: dec neck edge on alt rows 20(23:25) sts, ending with a purl row.

Work 1 row, ending at armhole edge.

Shape shoulder

Cast off 5 sts beg next and foll alt row.

Work 1 row.

Next row: cast off 5(6:7) sts, work to end.

Work 1 row.

Cast off.

Place 29(29:31) sts on holder.

Rejoin yarn to rem sts at neck edge, work to end.

Work rows 136 to end, reversing shapings.

SLEEVES (make 2)

Using 2¾mm (US 2) needles and M, cast on 87(89:91) sts and work 3cm (1¼in) in k1, p1 rib.

Change to 3¼mm (US 3) circular needle and patt as on Back.

Inc each end of 3rd and every foll 4th row to 97(99:101) sts.

Cont without shaping until completion of row 34, ending with a knit row.

Shape sleevehead

Cast off 4(5:6) sts beg next 2 rows.

Dec each end of next 4 rows.

Dec each end of next and every foll alt row to 51 sts.

Dec each end of next 6 rows.

Cast off 3 sts beg next 4 rows.

Cast off.

NECKBAND

Join right shoulder seam.

With RS facing and using 2¾mm (US 2) needles and M, pick up and knit 23 sts down left front neck, 29(29:31) sts from holder, 23 sts up right front neck and 51(51:53) sts from back neck.

Work 7 rows in k1, p1 rib.

Cast off loosely.

FINISHING

Join right shoulder seam and neckband. Join side seams and sleeve seams. Ease sleevehead into armhole and stitch into position. Weave in any loose ends.

Fluffy sweater

PICTURED ON PAGE 30

SIZES

	Small	Medium	Large
to fit bust (cm)	81-86	88-94	96-102
to fit bust (in)	(32-34)	(35-37)	(38-40)
actual size	91 (36)	99 (39)	107 (42)
back length	51 (20)	51 (20)	51 (20)
sleeve seam	46 (18)	46 (18)	46 (18)

MATERIALS

Rowan kid soft 50g balls:

desire	7	7	8

1 pair each 4½mm (US 7) and 5½mm (US 9) needles

Stitch holder

TENSION

16 sts and 22 rows = 10cm (4in) square over st st using Rowan kid soft and 5½mm (US 9) needles.

ABBREVIATIONS

See page 67.

T2 = twist 2 sts: knit the 2nd st and then the 1st st.

BACK

Using 4½mm (US 7) needles, cast on 73(77:81) sts and work in rib as folls:

Row 1: *p2, T2; rep from * to last st, p1.

Row 2: k1, *p2, k2; rep from * to end.

Rep rows 1 and 2 until work measures 7cm (2¾in), ending with row 2.

Change to 5½mm (US 9) needles and st st, inc each end of 11th and every foll 12th row to 79(83:87) sts.

Cont without shaping until work measures 28cm (11in), ending with a WS row.

Shape armholes

Rows 1-2: cast off 2(3:4) sts, work to end.

Rows 3: k2, sl1, k1, psso, knit to last 4 sts, k2tog, k2.

Row 4: purl.

Rep rows 3-4 until 67(69:71) sts rem.

Cont without shaping until work measures 49cm (19¼in), ending with a WS row.

Shape shoulders and neck

Cast off 6 sts, k16(17:18), cast off 23 sts, knit to end.

Working on 22(23:24) sts:

Row 1: cast off 6 sts, work to end.

Row 2: cast off 3 sts, work to end.

Row 3: cast off 6 sts, work to end.

Row 4: cast off 2 sts, work to end.

Row 5: cast off.

Rejoin yarn to rem sts at neck edge and work rows 2-5 again.

FRONT

Work as Back to 10 rows less than Back at shoulder shaping, ending with a WS row.

Shape neck

k26(27:28), turn.

Working on these 26(27:28) sts, dec neck edge on next 9 rows.

Shape shoulder

Cast off 6 sts beg of next and foll alt row.

Work 1 row.

Cast off.

Place 15 sts on holder.

Rejoin yarn to rem sts at neck edge, knit to end.

Work to match first side.

SLEEVES (make 2)

Using 4½mm (US 7) needles, cast on 41 sts and work 5cm (2in) in rib as on Back, ending with row 2.

Change to 5½mm (US 9) needles and st st.

Work 2 rows.

Row 3: k2, inc, knit to last 4 sts, inc, k3.

Cont, inc each end as set on every foll 8th row to 57(59:61) sts.

Cont, without shaping, until work measures 46cm (18in), ending with a WS row.

Shape sleevehead

Cast off 2(3:4) sts beg next 2 rows.

Row 3: k2, sl1, k1, psso, knit to last 4 sts, k2tog, k2.

Row 4: purl.

Rep rows 3-4 until 35 sts rem.

Cast off 4 sts beg next 4 rows.

Cast off.

NECKBAND

Join right shoulder seam.

With RS facing and using 4½mm (US 7) needles, pick up and knit 14 sts down side front neck, 15 sts from holder, 15 sts up side front neck and 37 sts from back neck.

Work 6 rows in rib as on Back welt, starting with row 2.

Cast off loosely in rib.

FINISHING

Join left shoulder seam and neckband. Join side seams. Join sleeve seams. Ease sleevehead into armhole and stitch in place. Weave in any loose ends.

Long-sleeved striped sweater

PICTURED ON PAGE 32

SIZES

	Small	Medium	Large
to fit bust cm (in)	81 (32)	86 (34)	91 (36)
actual size	86 (34)	91 (36)	96 (38)
back length	54 (21¼)	54 (21¼)	54 (21¼)
sleeve seam	46 (18)	46 (18)	46 (18)

MATERIALS

Rowan wool cotton 50g balls:

riviera (A)	4	4	5
citron (B)	3	3	3
gypsy (C)	3	3	4
tulip (D)	3	3	3

1 pair each 3¼mm (US 3) and 4mm (US 6) needles
Stitch holder

TENSION

22 sts and 30 rows = 10cm (4in) square over st st
using Rowan wool cotton and 4mm (US 6) needles.

ABBREVIATIONS

See page 67.

BACK

Using 3¼mm (US 3) needles and A, cast on 93(99:105)
sts and work 6cm (2½in) in k1, p1 rib.
Change to 4mm (US 6) needles and st st and
work as folls:

Rows 1-4: B.

Rows 5-6: C.

Rows 7-24: work as rows 1-6 three times, inc
each end of row 15.

Rows 25-28: D.

Rows 29-30: C.

Rows 31-48: work as rows 25-30 three times,
inc each end of row 35.

Rows 49-52: A.

Rows 53-54: C.

Rows 55-72: work as rows 49-54 three times,
inc each end of row 55.

These 72 rows form stripe rep.

Work rows 1-8 again.

Shape armholes

Rows 9-10: cast off 2(3:4) sts, work to end.

Rows 11-20: Dec each end of alt rows to
87(89:93) sts.

Cont without shaping to completion of row 64.

Shape neck and shoulders

Rows 65-66: cast off 6 sts, patt to end.

Row 67: cast off 6 sts, patt 17(18:19), cast off
29(29:31) sts, patt to end.

Row 68: cast off 6 sts, patt to end.

Row 69: cast off 3 sts, patt to end.

Row 70: cast off 6 sts, patt to end.

Row 71: cast off 2 sts, patt to end.

Row 72: cast off.

Rejoin yarns to rem sts at neck edge and work
rows 69-72 again.

FRONT

Work as Back to completion of 72 rows stripe rep.
Work rows 1-50 again, including armhole shaping.

Shape neck

Row 51: patt 34(35:36) sts, turn.

Working on these 34(35:36) sts:

Rows 52-58: dec neck edge, patt.

Rows 59-64: dec neck edge on alt rows.
24(25:26) sts.

Shape shoulder

Row 65: cast off 6 sts, patt to end.

Row 66: patt.

Rows 67-70: work as rows 65-66 twice.

Row 71: cast off.

Place 19(19:21) sts on holder.

Rejoin yarns to rem sts at neck edge, patt to end.

Work to match first side.

SLEEVES

Using 3¼mm (US 3) needles and A, cast on 49(51:53)
sts and work 5cm (2in) in k1, p1 rib.
Change to 4mm (US 6) needles, st st and stripe patt as
on Back, starting on row 31 and inc each end of 7th
and every foll 7th row to 77(79:81) sts.
Cont to completion of row 72, then work
rows 1-8 again.

Shape sleevehead

Cast off 2(3:4) sts beg next 2 rows.
Dec each end of next 6 rows.
Dec each end of next and every foll alt row to 41 sts.
Dec each end of next 4 rows.
Cast off 3 sts beg next 4 rows.
Cast off.

NECKBAND

Join right shoulder seam.
With RS facing and using 3¼mm (US 3) needles and A,
pick up and knit 21 sts down left front neck, 19(19:21)
sts from holder, 21 sts up right front neck and
39(39:41) sts from back neck.
Work 5 rows in k1, p1 rib.
Cast off loosely.

FINISHING

Join right shoulder seam and neckband. Join side seams
and sleeve seams. Ease sleevehead into armhole and
stitch into position. Weave in any loose ends.

Short-sleeved striped cotton sweater

PICTURED ON PAGE 34

SIZES

	Small	Medium	Large
to fit bust cm (in)	81 (32)	86 (34)	91 (36)
actual size	88 (35)	94 (37)	99 (39)
back length	51 (20)	51 (20)	51 (20)
sleeve seam	13 (5)	13 (5)	13 (5)

MATERIALS

Rowan handknit dk cotton 50g balls:

rosso (A)	3	3	3
gooseberry (B)	1	1	1
sugar (C)	3	3	3
flame (D)	2	2	2

1 pair each 3¼mm (US 3) and 4mm (US 6) needles
Stitch holder

TENSION

20 sts and 28 rows = 10cm (4in) square over st st using Rowan handknit dk cotton and 4mm (US 6) needles.

ABBREVIATIONS

See page 67.

BACK

Using 3¼mm (US 3) needles and A, cast on 81(87:93) sts and work 6cm (2½in) in k1, p1 rib.

Change to 4mm (US 6) needles and st st and work stripe patt as folls:

Rows 1-2: B.

Rows 3-16: C, inc each end of row 15.

Rows 17-18: B.

Rows 19-32: D, inc each end of row 29.

Rows 33-34: B.

Rows 35-48: A, inc each end of row 43.

These 48 rows form stripe rep.

Work rows 1-22 again, inc each end of row 7. 89(95:101) sts.

Shape armholes

Rows 23-24: cast off 2(3:4) sts, work to end.

Keeping patt correct, dec each end of next and every foll alt row to 73(75:77) sts.

Cont without shaping until armhole measures 19cm (7½in), ending with a WS row. Note patt row.

Shape neck and shoulders

Row 1: cast off 7 sts, patt 15(16:17), turn.

Row 2: dec, patt to end.

Row 3: cast off 7 sts, patt to last 2 sts, dec.

Row 4: work as row 2.

Row 5: cast off.

Rejoin yarns to rem sts at neck edge, cast off 29 sts, patt to end and work to match.

FRONT

Work as Back to 14 rows less than Back at neck and shoulder shaping (noted patt row).

Shape neck

Row 1: patt 29(30:31) sts, turn.

Rows 2-7: dec neck edge, patt.

Rows 8-14: dec neck edge on alt rows. 20(21:22) sts.

Row 15: cast off 7 sts, patt to last 2 sts, dec.

Row 16: patt.

Row 17: cast off 7 sts, patt to end.

Row 18: patt.

Row 19: cast off.

Place 15 sts on holder.

Rejoin yarns to rem sts at neck edge, patt to end.

Work rows 2-14 as before.

Row 15: dec, patt to end.

Row 16: cast off 7 sts, patt to end.

Row 17: patt.

Rows 18-19: work as rows 16-17.

Row 20: cast off.

SLEEVES

Using 3¼mm (US 3) needles and A, cast on 57(59:61) sts and work 5cm (2in) in k1, p1 rib.

Change to 4mm (US 6) needles, st st and stripe patt as on Back.

Inc each end of every 3rd row to 69(71:73) sts.

Cont to completion of row 22.

Shape sleevehead

Cast off 2(3:4) sts beg next 2 rows.

Dec each end of next 4 rows.

Dec each end of next and every foll alt row to 51 sts.

Work 1 row.

Dec each end of next and every foll 4th row to 41 sts.

Work 3 rows.

Dec each end of next 6 rows.

Cast off 3 sts beg next 4 rows.

Cast off.

NECKBAND

Join right shoulder seam.

With RS facing and using 3¼mm (US 3) needles and A, pick up and knit 18 sts down left front neck, 15 sts from holder, 18 sts up right front neck and 37 sts from back neck.

Work 5 rows in k1, p1 rib.

Cast off loosely in rib.

FINISHING

Join left shoulder seam and neckband. Join side seams. Join sleeve seams. Ease sleevehead into armhole and stitch into place. Weave in any loose ends.

Mittens with cabled ribs

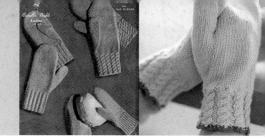

PICTURED ON PAGE 36

SIZES

Small-Medium   Medium-Large

MATERIALS

Rowan wool cotton 50g balls:

2 balls of citron (M) and small amount of contrast,

flower (C)

1 pair 3¼mm (US 3) needles

Cable needle

TENSION

24 sts and 32 rows = 10cm (4in) square over st st

using Rowan wool cotton and 3¼mm (US 3) needles.

ABBREVIATIONS

See page 67.

RIGHT MITTEN

Cuff

Using 3¼mm (US 3) needles and C, cast on 54 sts.

Change to M and work cable rib as folls:

Row 1 (RS): *p1, k4, p1; rep from * to end.

Row 2: *k1, p4, k1; rep from * to end.

Row 3: *p1, c4b, p1; rep from * to end.

Row 4: as row 2.

Rows 5-16: as rows 1-4 three times.

Rows 17-19: as rows 1-3.

Row 20: *patt 3, dec, patt 4; rep from

* to end. 48 sts.

Change to st st and work 4 rows.

Shape gusset for thumb

Row 1: k25, m1, k2, m1, k21.

Work 2 rows.

Row 4: p21, mp, p4, mp, p25.

Work 2 rows.

Cont, inc 2 sts on next and every 3rd row, working 2

extra sts between incs to row 18.

Row 19: k25, m1, k14, m1, k21. 62 sts.

Work 3 rows.

Shape thumb

Row 1: k41, turn.

Row 2: cast on 1 st, p17, turn.

Row 3: cast on 1 st, k18, turn.

Cont on these 18 sts until thumb measures 5cm (2in)

ending with a purl row.

Next row: *k1, k2tog; rep from * to end.

Next row: purl.

Next row: [k2tog] to end.

Break yarn and thread through rem sts. Draw up tightly

and secure.

Sew thumb seam.

With RS facing, rejoin yarn to base of thumb.

Pick up and knit 2 sts from cast on sts at beg of

thumb, knit across rem 21 sts. 48 sts.

Cont in st st until work measures 13(15)cm (5(6)in)

from top of cable rib, ending with a purl row.

Shape top

Row 1: *sl1, k1, psso, k20, k2tog; rep from * twice.

Row 2: purl.

Row 3: *sl1, k1, psso, k18, k2tog; rep from * twice.

Row 4: purl.

Cont decs as set on alt rows until 24 sts rem.

Work 1 row.

Cast off.

Sew top and side seam.

LEFT MITTEN

Cuff

Using 3¼mm (US 3) needles and C, cast on 54 sts.

Change to M and work cable rib as folls:

Row 1 (RS): *p1, k4, p1; rep from * to end.

Row 2: *k1, p4, k1; rep from * to end.

Row 3: *p1, c4b, p1; rep from * to end.

Row 4: as row 2.

Rows 5-16: as rows 1-4 three times.

Rows 17-19: as rows 1-3.

Row 20: *patt 3, dec, patt 4; rep from * to end. 48 sts.

Change to st st and work 4 rows.

Shape gusset for thumb

Row 1: k21, m1, k2, m1, k25.

Work 2 rows.

Row 4: p25, mp, p4, mp, p21.

Work 2 rows.

Cont incs as set to row 18.

Row 19: k21, m1, k14, m1, k25. 62 sts.

Work 3 rows.

Shape thumb

Row 1: k37, turn.

Row 2: cast on 1 st, p17, turn,

Row 3: cast on 1 st, k18, turn.

Complete thumb as for Right Mitten.

With RS facing, rejoin yarn to base of thumb.

Pick up and knit 2 sts from cast on sts at beg of thumb, knit across rem 25 sts.

Cont in st st until work measures 13(15)cm (5(6)in) from top of cable rib, ending with a purl row.

Shape top

Row 1: *sl1, k1, psso, k20, k2tog; rep from * twice.

Row 2: purl.

Row 3: *sl1, k1, psso, k18, k2tog; rep from * twice.

Row 4: purl.

Cont decs as set on alt rows until 24 sts rem.

Work 1 row.

Cast off.

Sew top and side seam.

Lace cardigan

PICTURED ON PAGE 38

SIZE

to fit bust cm (in)	81-88 (32-35)
actual size	91 (36)
back length	51 (20)
sleeve seam	48 (19)

MATERIALS

Rowan Cotton Glacé 50g balls:

hyacinth (M)	10
candy floss (C)	1

1 pair each 2¾mm (US 2) and 3¼mm (US 3) needles

5 buttons

TENSION

24 sts and 30 rows = 10cm (4in) square over st st using Rowan Cotton Glacé and 3¼mm (US 3) needles.

ABBREVIATIONS

See page 67.

BACK

Using 2¾mm (US 2) needles and C, cast on 99 sts.

Change to M and work 8cm (3in) in k1, p1 rib.

Change to 3¼mm (US 3) needles and patt as folls:

Row 1 (RS): *k1b, p1, k1b, k3, yo, sl1, k2tog, psso, yo, k3; rep from * to last 3 sts, k1b, p1, k1b.

Row 2 and alt rows: *[p1b, k1] twice, p7, k1; rep from * to last 3 sts, p1b, k1, p1b.

Row 3: *k1b, p1, k1b, k2, k2tog, yo, k1, yo, sl1, k1, psso, k2; rep from * to last 3 sts, k1b, p1, k1b.

Row 5: *k1b, p1, k1b, k1, k2tog, yo, k3, yo, sl1, k1, psso, k1; rep from * to last 3 sts, k1b, p1, k1b.

Row 7: *k1b, p1, k1b, k2tog, yo, k5, yo, sl1, k1, psso; rep from * to last 3 sts, k1b, p1, k1b.

Row 8: work as row 2.

These 8 rows form patt rep.

Cont in patt, inc each end of next and every foll 8th row to 109 sts, working extra sts into patt.

Cont without shaping to completion of 9th patt rep.

Shape armholes

Cast off 4 sts beg next 2 rows.

Dec each end next 4 rows.

Dec each end of next and every foll alt row to 87 sts.

Cont without shaping to completion of 16th patt rep.

Shape shoulders and neck

Rows 1-4: cast off 6 sts, work to end.

Row 5: cast off 6 sts, k8, cast off 35 sts, patt to end.

Row 6: cast off 6 sts, p6, p2tog.

Row 7: k2tog, k5.

Row 8: cast off.

Rejoin yarn to rem sts at neck edge and work to match.

LEFT FRONT

Using 2¾mm (US 2) needles and C, cast on 51 sts.

Change to M and work 8cm (3in) in k1, p1 rib, inc at end of last row. 52 sts.

Change to 3¼mm (US 3) needles and patt as folls:

Row 1 (RS): *k1b, p1, k1b, k3, yo, sl1, k2tog, psso, yo, k3; rep from * to last 4 sts, [k1b, p1] twice.

This sets patt as on Back, inc beg of 9th and every foll 8th row to 57 sts working extra sts into patt.

Cont without shaping to completion of 8th patt rep.

V-neck shaping

Row 1 (RS): patt to last 6 sts, k2tog, [k1b, p1] twice.

Row 2: *k1, p1b; rep from * twice, k1, patt to end.

Dec as set to completion of 9th patt rep, ending with a WS row. 53 sts.

Shape armhole

Keeping neck decs as set, cast off 4 sts, work to end.

Dec armhole edge on next 4 rows.

Dec armhole edge on foll 3 alt rows AT THE SAME TIME change neck decs to every foll 4th row from previous dec. Cont to completion of 16th patt rep, ending with a WS row. 27 sts.

Shape shoulder

Row 1: cast off 6 sts, patt to last 6 sts, k2tog, [k1b, p1] twice.

Row 2: work across sts.

Rows 3-6: work as rows 1-2 twice.

Row 7: cast off.

RIGHT FRONT

Cast on and rib as for Left Front.

Change to 3¼mm (US 3) needles and patt.

Row 1 (RS): [p1, k1b] twice, *k3, yo, sl1, k2tog, psso, yo, k3, k1b, p1, k1b; rep from * to end.

This sets patt as on Back.

Inc end of 9th and every foll 8th row to 57 sts.

Cont without shaping to completion of 8th patt rep.

V-neck shaping

Row 1 (RS): [p1, k1b] twice, sl1, k1, psso, patt to end.

Row 2: patt to last 5 sts, [k1, p1b] twice, k1.

Cont with neck shaping as set and work to match Left Front, reversing shaping by ending with a RS row before working armhole and shoulder.

SLEEVES (make 2)

Using 2¾mm (US 2) needles and C, cast on 51 sts.

Change to M and work 8cm (3in) in k1, p1 rib.

Change to 3¼mm (US 3) needles and patt as on Back.

Inc each end of 3rd and every foll 6th row to 83 sts.

Cont without shaping until work measures 48cm (19in), ending with a WS row.

Shape sleevehead

Cast off 4 sts beg next 2 rows.

Dec each end next 4 rows.

Dec each end of next and every foll alt row to 59 sts.

Work 1 row.

Dec each end of next and every foll 4th row to 49 sts.

Work 1 row.

Dec each end of next 6 rows.

Cast off 3 sts beg next 4 rows.

Cast off.

BUTTONBAND

Using 2¾mm (US 2) needles and M, cast on 7 sts and work in k1, p1 rib.

Make buttonholes by rib 3, yo, rib 2tog, rib 2 at 1cm (½in) and then 4 more at 6cm (2½in) intervals.

Cont in rib until band fits up right front, round back neck and down left front.

Cast off.

FINISHING

Join shoulder and side seams. Join sleeve seams. Ease sleevehead into armhole and stitch into position. Attach front band to cardigan. Sew on buttons to match buttonholes. Weave in any loose ends.

Fairisle gloves

PICTURED ON PAGE 40

SIZES

Small-Medium   Medium-Large

MATERIALS

Rowan 4-ply Botany 50g balls:

1 ball each, chrome (M), mocha, grape, tuscan, redwood and strawberry (C).

1 set of 4 x 2¾mm (US 2) double-ended needles

Spare needles

Safety pin

TENSION

32 sts and 36 rows = 10cm (4in) square over st st using Rowan 4-ply Botany and 2¾mm (US 2) needles.

ABBREVIATIONS

See page 67.

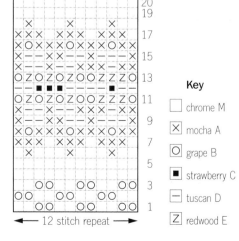

← 12 stitch repeat →

Key

☐ chrome M
☒ mocha A
Ⓞ grape B
◼ strawberry C
⊟ tuscan D
☑ redwood E

RIGHT GLOVE

Using 2¾mm (US 2) double-ended needles and C, cast on 60 sts (20 sts on each of 3 needles).

Change to M and work in rounds of k1, p1 rib until work measures 6cm (2½in).

Inc row: *rib 2, inc, rib 2; rep from * to end. 72 sts.

Work rounds 1-20 from chart and then 1-4 again. **

Round 5: place first 18 sts on safety pin for thumb, cast on 6 sts, complete the round.

Work rounds 6-20 from chart and then 1-5 again.

Divide for fingers

First finger

Slip the last 11 sts of round onto spare needle.

Using M, k5, cast on 2 sts, k11 from spare needle.

Divide these 18 sts onto 3 needles and knit 24(30) rounds.

Shape top

Round 1: [k2tog] 9 times.

Round 2: knit.

Round 3: [k1, k2tog] 3 times.

Break yarn leaving an end to run through the sts, draw up tightly and fasten off.

Second finger

With RS facing, rejoin M and k8, cast on 2 sts, knit the last 8 sts of the round, then pick up and knit 2 sts from the base of the first finger. Divide these 20 sts onto 3 needles and knit 28(34) rounds.

Shape top

Round 1: [k2tog] 10 times.

Round 2: knit

Round 3: [k2tog] 5 times.

Break yarn leaving an end to run through the sts, draw up tightly and fasten off.

Third finger

With RS facing, rejoin M and k7, cast on 2 sts, knit the last 7 sts of the round, then pick up and knit 2 sts from the base of the second finger.

Divide these 18 sts onto 3 needles and knit 24(30) rounds.

Shape top as first finger.

Fourth finger

With RS facing, rejoin M and k14 and pick up and knit 2 sts from the base of the third finger.

Divide these 16 sts onto 3 needles and knit 20(26) rounds.

Shape top

Round 1: [k2tog] 8 times.

Round 2: knit.

Round 3: [k2tog, k1] twice, k2tog.

Break yarn leaving an end to run through the sts, draw up tightly and fasten off.

Fairisle beret

Thumb

With RS facing, rejoin M and k18 from safety pin and pick up and knit 6 sts from base of thumb. Divide these 24 sts onto 3 needles and work 20(24) rounds.

Shape top

Round 1: [k2tog] 12 times.

Round 2: knit.

Round 3: [k2tog] 6 times.

Break yarn leaving an end to run through the sts, draw up tightly and fasten off.

LEFT GLOVE

Work as given for Right Glove to **.

Round 5: Patt 54, place next 18 sts on safety pin, cast on 6 sts.

Work rounds 6-20 from chart and then 1-5 again.

Divide for fingers

First finger

Slip the last 5 sts of round onto spare needle.

Using M, k11, cast on 2 sts, k5 from spare needle.

Complete as for Right Glove.

PICTURED ON PAGE 40

SIZE

To fit average head, 56cm (20in) circumference.

MATERIALS

Rowan 4-ply Botany 50g balls:

1 ball each, chrome (M), mocha (A), grape (B), strawberry (C), tuscan (D) and redwood (E).

1 pair each 2¾mm (US 2) and 3¼mm (US 3) needles.

TENSION

32 sts and 36 rows = 10cm (4in) square over st st using Rowan 4-ply Botany and 2¾mm (US 2) needles.

ABBREVIATIONS

See page 67.

BERET

Using 2¾mm (US 2) needles and C, cast on 144 sts.

Change to M and work 10 rows in k1, p1 rib.

Change to 3¼mm (US 3) needles and st st and work as folls:

Inc row: *inc, k1; rep from * to end. 216 sts.

Work 3 rows.

Rows 1-20: work from chart.

Work rows 1-4 again.

Row 5: *k2tog, k4; rep from * to end. 180 sts.

Work rows 6-18 again.

Row 19: *k2tog, k3; rep from * to end. 144 sts.

Work row 20, then rows 1-4 again.

Row 5: *k2tog, k2; rep from * to end. 108 sts.

Work rows 6-8 again.

Row 9: *1A, 3D, 2A, 2togD, 1A, 2togD, 1A; rep from * to end. 90 sts.

Row 10: *[1A, 1D] twice, 3A, 1D, 2A; rep from * to end.

Row 11: *1B, 3E, 2B, [1E, 1B] twice; rep from * to end.

Row 12: *1D, 3C, 3D, 1C, 2D; rep from * to end.

Row 13: 1B, *3E, 2togB, 1B, 1E, 1B, 2togE; rep from * to last 9 sts, 3E, 2togB, [1E, 1B] twice. 73 sts.

Row 14: *[1A, 1D] 3 times, 2D; rep from * to last st, 1A.

Row 15: *1A, sl1, 2togD, psso, [1A, 1D] twice; rep from * to last st, 1A. 55 sts.

Row 16: *2A, 1B; rep from * to last st, 1A.

Row 17: Using A, [k2tog] to last st, k1. 28 sts.

Row 18: [p2tog] to end. 14 sts.

Break yarn leaving thread for sewing. Weave in any loose ends. Thread yarn through rem sts, pull tight and secure. Sew seam.

Cotton twinset, cardigan

Classic twinset in 4 sizes

PICTURED ON PAGE 42

SIZES

	Small	Medium	Large
to fit bust cm (in)	81 (32)	86 (34)	91 (36)
actual size	86 (34)	91 (36)	96 (38)
back length	48 (18¾)	48 (18¾)	50 (19¾)
sleeve seam	46 (18)	46 (18)	46 (18)

MATERIALS

Rowan Cotton Glacé 50g balls:

poppy (M)	8	8	9
candy floss (C)	1	1	1

for the sweater: see overleaf

for the twinset (for the sweater, see overleaf): 13(13:15) balls of poppy (M) and 1 of candy floss (C).

1 pair each 2¾mm (US 2) and 3¼mm (US 3) needles

4 buttons

TENSION

24 sts and 30 rows = 10cm (4in) square over st st using Rowan Cotton Glacé and 3¼mm (US 3) needles.

ABBREVIATIONS

See page 67.

BACK

Using 2¾mm (US 2) needles and C, cast on 95(101:107) sts.

Change to M and knit 1 row.

Work 7cm (2¾in) in k1, p1 rib.

Change to 3¼mm (US 3) needles and st st.

Make fully-fashioned incs each end of 3rd and every foll 8th row to 105(111:117) sts by k2, inc, knit to last 4 sts, inc, k3.

Cont without shaping until work measures 27(27:29)cm (10½(10½:11½)in), ending with a WS row.

Shape armholes

Cast off 3(4:5) sts beg next 2 rows.

Dec each end next 4 rows.

Dec each end of next and every foll alt row to 83(87:91) sts.

Cont without shaping until work measures 46(46:48)cm (18(18:19)in), ending with a WS row.

Shape shoulders and neck

Rows 1-4: cast off 6 sts, work to end.

Row 5: cast off 6(7:7) sts, k6(6:7), cast off 35(37:39) sts, knit to end.

Row 6: cast off 6(7:7) sts, p4(4:5), p2tog.

Row 7: k2tog, k3(3:4).

Row 8: cast off.

Rejoin yarn to rem sts at neck edge and work to match.

LEFT FRONT

Using 2¾mm (US 2) needles and C, cast on 47(49:53) sts.

Change to M and knit 1 row.

Work 7cm (2½in) in k1, p1 rib.

Change to 3¼mm (US 3) needles and st st.

Make fully-fashioned incs as on Back at beg of 3rd and every foll 8th row to 52(54:58) sts.

Cont without shaping until work measures 20cm (8in), ending with a WS row.

V-neck shaping

Knit to last 3 sts, k2tog, k1.

Cont dec neck edge on every foll 4th row as set and AT THE SAME TIME when the work measures 27(27:29)cm (10½(10½:11½)in), ending with a WS row.

Shape armhole

Keeping neck decs as set, cast off 3(4:5) sts, work to end.

Dec armhole edge on next 4 rows.

Dec armhole edge on foll 4 alt rows.

Cont with neck decs until 22(23:24) sts rem.

Cont without shaping until work measures 46(46:48)cm (18(18:19)in), ending with a WS row.

Shape shoulder

Row 1: cast off 6 sts, work to end.

Row 2: work to end.

Rows 3-4: work as rows 1-2.

Row 5: cast off 6(7:7) sts, work to end.

Row 6: work as row 2.

Row 7: cast off.

RIGHT FRONT

Cast on and rib as for Left Front.

Change to 3¼mm (US 3) needles and st st.

Make fully-fashioned incs as on Back at end of 3rd and

every foll 8th row to 52(54:58) sts.

Cont without shaping until work measures 20cm (8in),

ending with a WS row.

V-neck shaping

K1, sl1, k1, psso, knit to end.

Cont with neck shaping as set and work to match Left

Front, reversing shapings by ending with a RS row

before armhole and shoulder shaping.

SLEEVES (make 2)

Using 2¾mm (US 2) needles and C, cast on

51(53:55) sts.

Change to M and knit 1 row.

Work 5cm (2in) in k1, p1 rib.

Change to 3¼mm (US 3) needles and st st.

Make fully-fashioned incs as on Back at each end of 3rd

and every foll 6th row to 79(81:85) sts.

Cont without shaping until work measures 46cm (18in),

ending with a WS row.

Shape sleevehead

Cast off 3(4:5) sts beg next 2 rows.

Dec each end next 4 rows.

Dec each end of next and every foll alt row to

59(59:61) sts.

Work 1 row.

Dec each end of next and every foll 4th row to

49(49:51) sts.

Work 1 row.

Dec each end of next 6 rows.

Cast off 3 sts beg next 4 rows.

Cast off.

FRONTBAND

Using 2¾mm (US 2) needles and M, cast on 7 sts and

work in k1, p1 rib.

Make buttonholes by rib 3, yo, rib 2tog, rib 2 at 1cm

(½in) and then 3 more at 6cm (2½in) intervals.

Cont in rib until band fits up right front, round back neck

and down left front.

Cast off.

FINISHING

Join shoulder and side seams. Join sleeve seams. Ease

sleevehead into armhole and stitch into position. Attach

front band to cardigan. Sew on buttons to match

buttonholes. Weave in any loose ends.

Cotton twinset, sweater

PICTURED ON PAGE 42

SIZES

	Small	Medium	Large
to fit bust cm (in)	81 (32)	86 (34)	91 (36)
actual size	86 (34)	91 (36)	96 (38)
back length	48 (18¾)	48 (18¾)	50 (19¾)
sleeve seam	12 (4¾)	12 (4¾)	12 (4¾)

MATERIALS

Rowan Cotton Glacé 50g balls:

poppy (M)	5	5	6
candy floss (C)	1	1	1

for the twinset (for the cardigan, see previous page):
13(13:15) balls of poppy (M) and 1 of candy floss (C).
1 pair each 2¾mm (US 2) and 3¼mm (US 3) needles
Stitch holder

TENSION

24 sts and 30 rows = 10cm (4in) square over st st
using Rowan Cotton Glacé and 3¼mm (US 3) needles.

ABBREVIATIONS

See page 67.

BACK

Using 2¾mm (US 2) needles and C, cast on
95(101:107) sts.
Change to M and knit 1 row.
Work 7cm (2¾in) in k1, p1 rib.
Change to 3¼mm (US 3) needles and st st.
Make fully-fashioned incs each end of 3rd and every foll
8th row to 105(111:117) sts by k2, inc, knit to
ast 4 sts, inc, k3.
Cont without shaping until work measures 27(27:29)cm
(10½(10½:11½)in), ending with a WS row.

Shape armholes

Cast off 3(4:5) sts beg next 2 rows.
Dec each end next 4 rows.
Dec each end of next and every foll alt row to
83(87:91) sts.
Cont without shaping until work measures 46(46:48)cm
(18(18:19)in), ending with a WS row.

Shape shoulders and neck

Rows 1-4: cast off 6 sts, work to end.
Row 5: cast off 6(7:7) sts, k6(6:7), cast off 35(37:39)
sts, knit to end.
Row 6: cast off 6(7:7) sts, p4(4:5), p2tog.
Row 7: k2tog, k3(3:4).
Row 8: cast off.
Rejoin yarn to rem sts at neck edge and work to match.

FRONT

Work as Back until work measures 41(41:43)cm
(16(16:17)in), ending with a WS row.

Shape neck

k32(33:34), turn.
Working on these sts:
Dec neck edge on next 7 rows.
Dec neck edge on next and every foll alt row to
22(23:24) sts.
Cont without shaping until work measures 46(46:48)cm
(18(18:19)in), ending with a WS row.

Shape shoulder

With RS facing, cast off 6 sts beg next and foll alt row.
Work 1 row.
Cast off 6(7:7) sts beg of next row.
Work 1 row.
Cast off.
Place 19(21:23) sts on holder.
Rejoin yarn to rem sts at neck edge, knit to end.
Work to match first side.

SLEEVES

Using 2¾mm (US 2) needles and C, cast on
73(75:77) sts.
Change to M and knit 1 row.
Work 4.5cm (1¾in) in k1, p1 rib.
Change to 3¼mm (US 3) needles and st st, inc each
end of 2nd and every foll 3rd row to 79(81:85) sts.

Cont without shaping until work measures 12cm (4¾in),
ending with a WS row.

Shape sleevehead

Cast off 3(4:5) sts beg next 2 rows.

Dec each end next 4 rows.

Dec each end of next and every foll alt row to
59(59:61) sts.

Work 1 row.

Dec each end of next and every foll 4th row to
49(49:51) sts.

Work 1 row.

Dec each end of next 6 rows.

Cast off 3 sts beg next 4 rows.

Cast off.

NECKBAND

Join right shoulder.

With RS facing and using 2¾mm (US 2) needles and M,
pick up and knit 22 sts down side front neck ,
19(21:23) sts from holder, 22 sts up side front neck
and 39(41:43) sts from back neck.

Work 5 rows in k1, p1 rib.

Cast off loosely.

FINISHING

Join neckband and left shoulder seam. Join side and
sleeve seams. Ease sleevehead into armhole and stitch
into place. Weave in any loose ends.

Short-sleeved lace sweater with ribbons

PICTURED ON PAGE 44

SIZE

to fit bust cm (in)	81-88 (32-35)
actual size	91 (36)
back length	51 (20)
sleeve seam	12 (4¾)

MATERIALS

Rowan 4-ply cotton 50g balls:

violet	7

1 pair each 2¾mm (US 2) and 3¼mm (US 3) needles
Cable needle
2m (2yd) of contrast ribbon 7mm (¼in) wide

TENSION

17 sts (1 patt rep) = 6cm (2¼ wide using Rowan 4-ply cotton and 3¼mm (US 3) needles.

ABBREVIATIONS

See page 67.

BACK

Using 2¾mm (US 2) needles, cast on 107 sts.

Work 6cm (2½in) in k1, p1 rib.

Change to 3¼mm (US 3) needles.

Inc row (WS): p3, [*p1, mp; rep from * 3 times, p11] 7 times, [p1, mp] 3 times, p3. 131 sts.

Change to patt as folls:

Row 1 (RS): *p2, k8, p2, p2tog, yo, k1, yo, p2tog; rep from * to last 12 sts, p2, k8, p2.

Row 2: *k2, p8, k3, p3, k1; rep from * to last 12 sts, k2, p8, k2.

Row 3: p2, c4b, c4f, *p1, p2tog, yo, k3, yo, p2tog, p1, c4b, c4f; rep from * to last 2 sts, p2.

Row 4: *k2, p8, k2, p5; rep from * to last 12 sts, k2, p8, k2.

Row 5: p2, *k8, p2tog, yo, k5, yo, p2tog; rep from * to last 10 sts, k8, p2.

Row 6: k2, *p8, k1, p7, k1; rep from * to last 10 sts, p8, k2.

Row 7: p2, *c4b, c4f, p1, yo, k2, sl1, k2tog, psso, k2, yo, p1; rep from * to last 10 sts, c4b, c4f, p2.

Row 8: work as row 6.

Row 9: *p2, k8, p2, yo, k1, sl1, k2tog, psso, k1, yo; rep from * to last 12 sts, p2, k8, p2.

Row 10: work as row 4.

Row 11: p2, *c4b, c4f, p3, yo, sl1, k2tog, psso, yo, p3; rep from * to last 10 sts, c4b, c4f, p2.

Row 12: work as row 2.

These 12 rows form patt rep.

Cont in patt, inc each end of next and every foll 12th row to 141 sts, working extra sts into patt.

Cont without shaping until work measures 29cm (11½in), ending with a WS row.

Shape armholes

Cast off 5 sts beg next 2 rows.

Dec at each end of next 6 rows.

Dec each end of next and every foll alt row to 113 sts.

Cont without shaping until work measures 47cm (18½in), ending with a RS row.

** **Next row:** patt 23, p5, [*p2tog; rep from * 3 times, p11] 3 times, [p2tog] 3 times, p5, patt 23.

Work eyelets for ribbon as folls:

Row 1: patt 23, k2, [cast off 2 sts, k5] 7 times, cast off 2 sts, k2, patt 23.

Row 2: patt 23, p2, [cast on 2 sts, p5] 7 times, cast on 2 sts, p2, patt 23. **

Shape shoulders and neck

Row 3: cast off 5 sts, patt 18, k55, patt 23.

Row 4: cast off 5 sts, patt 18, p5, cast off 45 sts, p5, patt 18.

Row 5: cast off 5 sts, patt 13, k5.

Row 6: p5, patt 13.

Row 7: cast off 8 sts, patt 5, k5.

Row 8: purl.

Row 9: cast off 5 sts.

Row 10: purl.

Row 11: cast off.

Rejoin yarn to rem sts at neck edge and work to match.

FRONT

Work as Back until work measures 42cm (16½in), ending with a RS row.

Work ** to ** as on Back.

Row 3: patt 23, k55, patt 23.

Row 4: patt 23, p5, cast off 45 sts, p5, patt 23.

On 28 sts and keeping patt correct with 5 sts in st st at neck edge work 4 more rows.

Row 9: make eyelet – patt 23, k1, cast off 2 sts, k2.

Row 10: p2, cast on 2 sts, p1, patt 23.

Cont until work measures same as Back at shoulder, making further eyelets every foll 7th and 8th rows, ending with WS row.

Shape shoulders

Keeping eyelet sequence correct, work as folls:

Row 1: cast off 5 sts, work to end.

Row 2 and alt rows: work across sts.

Row 3: work as row 1.

Row 5: cast off 8 sts, work to end.

Row 7: work as row 1.

Row 9: cast off.

Rejoin yarn to rem sts at neck edge and work to match.

SLEEVES (make 2)

Using 2¾mm (US 2) needles, cast on 79 sts and work 10 rows in k1, p1 rib.

Change to 3¼mm (US 3) needles and work as folls:

Row 1: knit.

Row 2: purl.

Row 3: k7 , *cast off 2 sts, k5; rep from * to last 2 sts, k2.

Row 4: p7, *cast on 2 sts, p5; rep from * to last 2 sts, p2.

Row 5: knit.

Row 6: p3, [*p1, mp; rep from * 3 times, p11] to last 6 sts, [p1, mp] 3 times, p3. 97 sts.

Change to patt

Row 1: *p2, k8, p2, p2tog, yo, k1, yo, p2tog; rep from * to last 12 sts, p2, k8, p2.

This sets patt as on Back.

Inc each end of next and every foll 3rd row to 111 sts.

Cont to completion of 2nd patt rep.

Shape sleevehead

3rd patt rep

Rows 1-2: cast off 5 sts, patt to end

Rows 3-12: dec each end of every row. 81 sts.

4th patt rep

Rows 1-2: dec each end of both rows.

Rows 3-12: dec each end of alt rows. 67 sts.

5th patt rep

Rows 1-8: dec each end of alt rows.

Rows 9-12: dec each end of every row. 51 sts.

6th patt rep

Rows 1-2: dec each end of every row.

Rows 3-5: cast off 4 sts, patt to end.

Row 6: cast off 4 sts, p2, k1, [p2tog] 4 times, k1, p7, k1, [p2tog] 4 times, k1, p2.

Row 7: cast off.

NECKBAND

Join right shoulder seam.

With RS facing, using 2¾mm (US 2) needles and M, pick up and knit 21 sts down left side front neck, 1 st from corner, 47 sts from centre front, 1 st from corner, 21 sts up right front neck, 8 sts down side back neck, 1 st from corner, 47 sts from centre back, 1 st from corner and 8 sts up side back neck. Work as folls:

Row 1: *k1, p1; rep from * 3 times, k1, p3, *k1, p1; rep from * 22 times, k1, p3, *k1, p1; rep from * 13 times, k1, p3, *k1, p1; rep from * 22 times, k1, p3, *k1, p1; rep from * 10 times.

Row 2: *k1, p1; rep from * 9 times, *k1, p2tog; rep from * twice, *k1, p1; rep from * 21 times, *k1, p2tog; rep from * twice, *k1 p1; rep from * 12 times, *k1, p2tog; rep from * twice, *k1, p1; rep from * 21 times, *k1, p2tog; rep from * twice, *k1, p1; rep from * 3 times.

Row 3: *k1, p1; rep from * twice, k1, p2tog; p1, p2togb, *k1, p1; rep from * 20 times, k1, p2tog, p1, p2togb, *k1, p1; rep from * 11 times, k1, p2tog, p1, p2togb, *k1, p1; rep from * 20 times, k1, p2tog, p1, p2togb, *k1, p1; rep from * 9 times.

Rows 4-5: dec as set.

Row 6: cast off in rib.

FINISHING

Join neckband and left shoulder seam. Weave in loose ends. Join side and sleeve seams. Stitch sleevehead into armhole. Thread ribbon through eyelets and tie into bow at neck edge. Stitch to required length on sleeves.

Short-sleeved wavy line sweater

PICTURED ON PAGE 46

SIZE

to fit bust cm (in)	81-89 (32-35)
actual size	91 (36)
back length	51 (20)
sleeve seam	12 (4¾)

MATERIALS

Rowan 4-ply Botany 50g balls:

chrome (M)	3
redwood (A)	2
mocha (B)	1
tuscan (C)	1

1 pair each 2¾mm (US 2) and 3¼mm (US 3) needles

TENSION

1 patt rep = 5.5cm (2¼in) wide using Rowan 4-ply Botany and 3¼mm (US 3) needles.

ABBREVIATIONS

See page 67.

BACK

Using M and 2¾mm (US 2) needles, cast on 117 sts and work 27 rows in k1, p1 rib.

Row 28: *rib 3, inc; rep from * to last st, rib 1. 146 sts.

Change to 3¼mm (US 3) needles and patt as folls:

Row 1 (RS): knit.

Row 2: k1, *k6, p6, k6; rep from * to last st, k1.

Row 3: k1, *[k2tog] 3 times, [k1, yo] 6 times, [k2tog] 3 times; rep from * to last st, k1.

Row 4: purl

These four rows form patt rep.

Cont in patt, colour changes only given.

Rows 5-6: B.

Rows 7-8: M.

Rows 9-10: B.

Rows 11-16: M.

Rows 17-24: A.

Rows 25-26: C.

Rows 27-28: M.

Rows 29-30: C.

Rows 31-38: A.

Rows 39-40: M.

Rep rows 1-40 again, then rows 1-6.

Shape armhole

Rows 7-8: cast off 18 sts, patt to end. **

Work rows 9-40, then 1-37 again.

Row 38: p29, cast off 52 sts, purl to end.

Shape shoulder

Work in st st and using M, cast off 6 sts beg of next and foll 3 alt rows.

Work 1 row.

Cast off.

Rejoin yarn to rem sts and work to match.

FRONT

Work as Back to **.

Work rows 9-40, then 1-16 again.

Shape neck

Row 17: k29, turn.

Row 18: p4, k12, p6, k7.

Row 19: k1, patt 18, [k2tog] 3 times, [k1, yo] 3 times, k1.

Row 20: purl.

Rows 21-38: patt as set.

Shape shoulder

Working in st st and using M, cast off 6 sts beg of next and foll 3 alt rows.

Work 1 row.

Cast off.

Rejoin M to rem sts and cast off centre 52 sts.

Break M.

Rejoin A to rem sts and knit to end (row 17).

Row 18: k7, p6, k12, p4.

Row 19: k1, [k1, yo] 3 times, [k2tog] 3 times,

patt 18, k1.

Row 20: purl.

Work to match first side.

SLEEVES (make 2)

Using 2¾mm (US 2) needles and M, cast on 81 sts.

Work 17 rows in k1, p1 rib.

Row 18: *inc, rib 7; rep from * to last st, inc. 92 sts.

Change to 3¼mm (US 3) needles and patt as on Back.

Work rows 17-40, then rows 1-30 placing markers at

each end of row 7.

Shape sleevehead

Rows 31-38: cast off 6 sts, patt to end.

Row 39: cast off.

NECKBAND

Join right shoulder seam.

With RS facing and using 2¾mm (US 2) needles and M,
pick up and knit 25 sts down left side front neck, 1 st
from corner, 49 sts from centre front, 1 st from corner,
25 sts up right front neck, 8 sts down side back neck,
1 st from corner, 49 sts from centre back, 1 st from
corner and 8 sts up side back neck. Work as folls:

Row 1: [k1, p1] 3 times, k1, p3, [k1, p1] 23 times,
k1, p3, [k1, p1] 15 times, k1, p3, [k1, p1] 23 times,
k1, p3, [k1, p1] 12 times.

Row 2: [k1, p1] 11 times, [k1, p2tog] twice, [k1, p1]
22 times, [k1, p2tog] twice, [k1, p1] 14 times, [k1,
p2tog] twice, [k1, p1] 22 times, [k1, p2tog] twice, [k1,
p1] 3 times.

Row 3: [k1, p1] twice, k1, p2tog, p1, p2togb, [k1, p1]
21 times, k1, p2tog, p1, p2togb, [k1, p1] 13 times, k1,
p2tog, p1, p2togb, [k1, p1] 21 times, k1, p2tog, p1,
p2togb, [k1, p1] 11 times.

Rows 4-5: dec as set.

Row 6: cast off in rib.

FINISHING

Join neckband and left shoulder seam. Weave in any
loose ends. Join side seams. Join sleeve seam to
markers. Ease sleevehead into armhole, placing remainder
of sleeve length across sts cast off at armhole and
stitch into position.

Fairisle cardigan

PICTURED ON PAGE 48

SIZES

	Small	Medium	Large
to fit bust cm (in)	81 (32)	86 (34)	91 (36)
actual size	86 (34)	91 (36)	96 (38)
back length	51 (20)	51 (20)	51 (20)
sleeve seam	45 (17¾)	45 (17¾)	45 (17¾)

MATERIALS

Rowan 4-ply Botany 50g balls:

chrome (M)	6	7	7

1 ball each grape (A), mocha and redwood (B).

1 pair each 2¾mm (US 2) and 3¼mm (US 3) needles

7 buttons

Safety pin

TENSION

28 sts and 36 rows = 10cm (4in) square over st st using Rowan 4-ply Botany and 3¼mm (US 3) needles.

ABBREVIATIONS

See page 67.

BACK

Using 2¾mm (US 2) needles and A, cast on 121(129:137) sts.

Change to M and work 6cm (2½in) in k1, p1 rib.

Change to 3¼mm (US 3) needles and st st and work as folls:

Rows 1-4: M.

Row 5: *1B, 3M; rep from * to last st, 1B.

Rows 6-9: M.

Row 10: *2M, 1B, 1M; rep from * to last st, 1M.

These 10 rows form patt rep.

Cont in patt to completion of row 84.

Shape armholes

Cont to work from chart (see overleaf)

Rows 85-86: cast off 4(5:6) sts, patt to end.

Rows 87-90: dec each end, patt.

Row 91-102: dec each end of alt rows, patt. 93(99:105 sts).

Rows 103-152: follow chart.

Shape shoulders and neck (keeping patt correct)

Rows 1-4: cast off 5 sts, patt to end.

Row 5: cast off 5 sts, patt 13(15:17), cast off 37(39:41) sts, patt to end.

Row 6: cast off 5 sts, patt to end.

Row 7: cast off 3 sts, patt to end.

Row 8: cast off 5 sts, patt to end.

Row 9: cast off 2 sts, patt to end.

Row 10: cast off.

Rejoin yarn to rem sts at neck edge and work rows 7-10.

LEFT FRONT

Using 2¾mm (US 2) needles and A, cast on 61(65:69) sts.

Change to M and work 6cm (2½in) in k1, p1 rib.

Change to 3¼mm (US 3) needles and st st and work 84 rows as on Back.

Shape armhole

Cont to work from chart.

Row 85: cast off 4(5:6) sts, work to end.

Row 86: purl.

Rows 87-90: dec armhole edge, patt.

Rows 91-102: dec armhole edge on alt rows, patt. 47(50:53) sts.

Rows 103-139: follow chart.

Shape neck

Row 140: cast off 10(11:12) sts, patt.

Rows 141-149: dec neck edge, patt.

Rows 150-152: dec neck edge on alt rows, patt.

Shape shoulder

Row 1: cast off 5 sts, patt to last 2 sts, k2tog.

Row 2: purl.

Rows 3-8: work as rows 1-2 three times.

Row 9: cast off.

RIGHT FRONT

Make as for Left Front, reversing shapings.

SLEEVES (make 2)

Using 2¾mm (US 2) needles and A, cast on 59 sts.

Change to M and work 5cm (2in) in k1, p1 rib.

Inc row: rib 2, *inc, rib 5; rep from * 9 times,

inc, rib 2. 69 sts.

Change to 3¼mm (US 3) needles, st st and

patt as on Back.

Inc each end of 3rd and every foll 8th(8th:7th)

row to 101(103:105) sts.

Cont without shaping to completion of row 144.

Shape sleevehead

Cont to work from chart.

Rows 145-146: cast off 4(5:6) sts, patt to end.

Rows 147-151: dec each end, patt.

Rows 151-180: dec each end of alt rows, patt.

55 sts.

Dec each end of next 6 rows.

Cast off 3 sts beg next 4 rows.

Cast off.

BUTTONBAND

Using 2¾mm (US 2) needles and M, cast on 9 sts.

Work in k1, p1 rib until work fits from hem to neck on

left front.

Break yarn.

Leave sts on safety pin.

Mark positions for buttons, the 1st and 2nd at 1cm

(½in) and 6cm (2½in) from hem, the 6th at 7.5cm (3in)

down from neck and the 3rd to 5th spaced evenly

between the 2nd and 6th.

BUTTONHOLE BAND

As button band, making buttonholes to match marked

positions by:

Row 1: rib 3, cast off 3 sts, rib 3.

Row 2: rib 3, cast on 3 sts, rib 3.

Do not break yarn.

Leave sts on needle.

NECKBAND

Join shoulder seams.

With RS facing and using 2¾mm (US 2) needles and M,

rib across buttonhole band, pick up and knit 30(31:32)

sts from right front neck, 47(49:51) sts from back neck,

30(31:32) sts from left front neck and rib across

button band.

Work 7 rows in k1, p1 rib making 7th buttonhole on

rows 4 and 5.

Cast off in rib.

FINISHING

Join side seams and sleeve seams. Ease sleevehead into

armhole and stitch into place. Attach button and

buttonhole bands to fronts. Weave in any loose ends.

Sew on buttons.

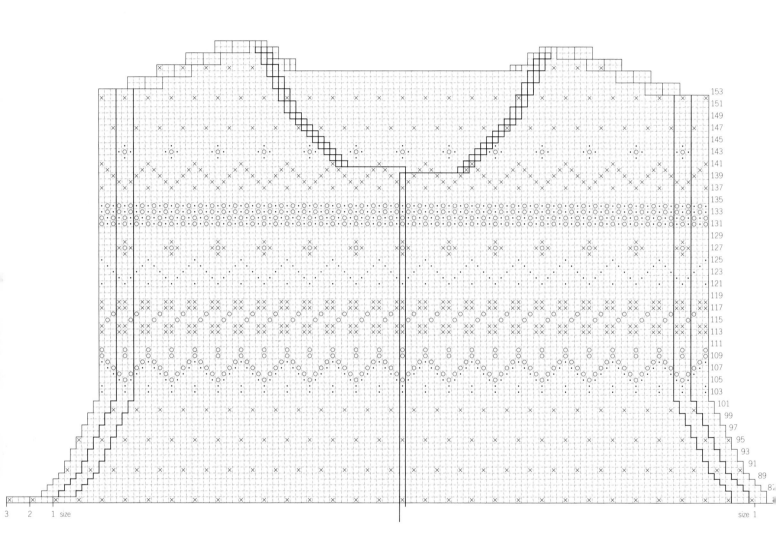

153
151
149
147
145
143
141
139
137
135
133
131
129
127
125
123
121
119
117
115
113
111
109
107
105
103
101
99
97
95
93
91
89
87

3   2   1 size

size 1

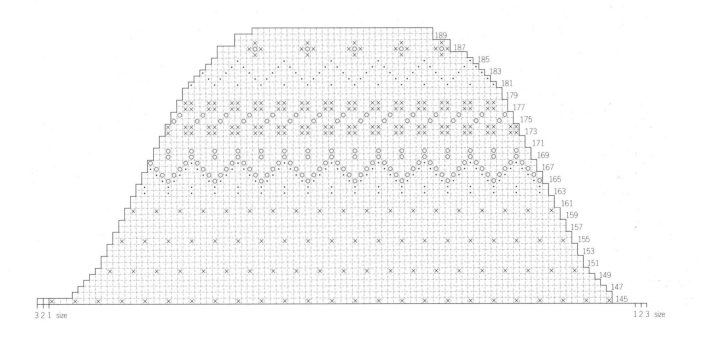

189
187
185
183
181
179
177
175
173
171
169
167
165
163
161
159
157
155
153
151
149
147
145

3 2 1 size

1 2 3 size

Key

☐ chrome

☒ redwood

⊡ mocha

⊙ grape

Silk ribbed vest

PICTURED ON PAGE 50

SIZES

	Small	Medium	Large
to fit bust (cm)	76-81	86	91
to fit bust (in)	(30-32)	(34)	(36)
actual size	81 (32)	86 (34)	91 (36)
centre back length	33 (13)	33 (13)	36 (14)

MATERIALS

Jaeger silk 50 g balls:

6 balls midnight (M) and 1 ball silver blue (C)

1 pair 2¾mm (US 2) needles

TENSION

26 sts and 38 rows = 10cm (4in) square over st st using Jaeger silk and 2¾mm (US 2) needles.

ABBREVIATIONS

See page 67.

BACK

Using 2¾mm (US 2) needles and M, cast on 110(115:120) sts and work 2cm (¾in) in k1, p1 rib.

Change to patt and work as folls:

Row 1 (RS): *k2, pl, k2; rep from * to end.

Row 2: *p2, kl, p2; rep from * to end.

Rep rows 1-2 until work measures 25(25:28)cm (10(10:11)in), ending with row 2.

Change to moss st and cont until work measures 30(30:33)cm (12(l2:13)in), ending with a WS row.

Shape armholes

Cast off 7(8:9) sts beg next 2 rows.

Dec each end of next 10 rows. 76(79:82) sts.

Next row: dec, moss 35(37:38), cast off 2(1:2) sts, moss st to last 2 sts, dec.

Working on 36(38:39) sts:

Row 1 (WS): dec neck edge.

Row 2: dec each end.

Rep rows 1-2 until 6(7:8) sts rem.

Cont on these 6(7:8) sts until moss section of work measures 23cm (9in).

Cast off.

Rejoin yarn to rem sts at centre front and work to match first side.

FRONT

Using 2¾mm (US 2) needles and M, cast on 110(115:120) sts and work 2cm (¾in) in k1, p1 rib.

Change to patt and work as folls:

Row 1 (RS): *k2, pl, k2; rep from * to end.

Row 2: *p2, kl, p2; rep from * to end.

Rep rows 1-2 until work measures 25(25:28)cm (10(10:11)in), ending with row 2.

Change to moss st and cont until work measures 30(30:33)cm (12(l2:13)in), ending with a WS row.

Shape armholes

Cast off 7(8:9) sts beg next 2 rows.

Dec each end of next 10 rows. 76(79:82) sts.

Next row: dec, moss 35(37:38), cast off 2(1:2) sts, moss st to last 2 sts, dec.

Working on 36(38:39) sts:

Row 1 (WS): dec neck edge.

Row 2: dec each end.

Rep rows 1-2 until 6(7:8) sts rem.

Cont on these 6(7:8) sts until moss section of work measures 23cm (9in).

Cast off.

Rejoin yarn to rem sts at centre front and work to match first side.

TRIMS

Join first shoulder seam.

Neck trim

Using 2¾mm (US 2) needles and C, with RS facing, pick up and knit 91 sts around back and 90 sts around front necks. 181 sts.

Next row: cast off 5 sts, *sl st on right needle back to left needle, cast on 2 sts, cast off 7 sts; rep from * to end. Fasten off.

Join second shoulder seam.

Arm trims

Using 2¾mm (US 2) needles and C, with RS facing, pick up and knit 117(121:125) sts around armhole.

Work as for neck trim.

FINISHING

Join side seams. Weave in any loose ends.

Long-sleeved bolero

PICTURED ON PAGE 52

SIZES

	Small	Medium	Large
to fit bust cm (in)	81 (32)	86 (34)	91 (36)
actual size	86 (34)	91 (36)	96 (38)
back length	41 (16)	41 (16)	42 (16½)
sleeve seam	46 (18)	46 (18)	46 (18)

MATERIALS

Rowan 4-ply Botany 50g balls:

jet	6	6	7

1 pair each 2¾mm (US 2) and 3¼mm (US 3) needles

TENSION

28 sts and 36 rows = 10cm (4in) square over st st using Rowan 4-ply Botany and 3¼mm (US 3) needles.

ABBREVIATIONS

See page 67.

BACK

Using 3¼mm (US 3) needles, cast on 108(116:124) sts and work 4 rows in st st.

Inc each end of next and every foll 8th row to 118(126:134) sts.

Cont without shaping until work measures 19(19:20)cm (7½(7½:8)in), ending with a purl row.

Shape armholes

Cast off 5(6:7) sts beg next 2 rows.

Dec each end of next 4 rows.

Dec each end of next and every foll alt row to 90(96:102) sts.

Cont without shaping until work measures 38(38:39)cm (15(15:15½)in), ending with a purl row.

Shape neck and shoulders

Cast off 5 sts beg next 4 rows.

Row 5: cast off 5 sts, k13(15:17), cast off 34(36:38) sts, knit to end.

Row 6: cast off 5 sts, work to end.

Row 7: cast off 3 sts, work to end.

Row 8: work as row 6.

Row 9: cast off 2 sts, work to end.

Row 10: cast off.

Rejoin yarn to rem sts at neck edge.

Work rows 7-10 again.

LEFT FRONT

Using 3¼mm (US 3) needles, cast on 24(28:32) sts and work in st st.

Shaping rows only given.

Rows 4, 6, 8, 10, 12 and 14 (front edge shaping): cast on 2 sts, purl all sts.

Rows 5 and 13 (side edge shaping): inc, knit to end.

Rows 16, 18, 20, 21, 22, 24, 26, 28, 29 and 30: inc, work to end.

Rows 34, 37, 38, 42 and 46: inc, work to end. 53(57:61) sts.

Cont without shaping until work measures 19(19:20)cm (7½(7½:8)in), ending with a purl row.

Shape armhole

Cast off 5(6:7) sts, work to end.

Work 1 row.

** Dec armhole edge on next 4 rows.

Dec armhole edge on next and every foll alt row to 39(42:45) sts.

Work 1 row.

Shape front neck

Dec neck edge on next and every foll 3rd row to 23(25:27) sts.

Cont without shaping until work measures 38(38:39)cm (15(15:15½)in), ending with a purl row.

Shape shoulders

Cast off 5 sts beg next and foll 3 alt rows.

Work 1 row.

Cast off. **

RIGHT FRONT

Using 3¼mm (US 3) needles, cast on 24(28:32) sts
and work in st st.

Shaping rows only given.

Row 3, 7, 9 and 11 (front edge shaping): cast
on 2 sts, knit all sts.

Row 5 and 13: cast on 2 sts, knit to last
2 sts, inc, k1.

Rows 15, 17, 19, 23, 25 and 27: inc,
knit to end.

Rows 21, 29 and 37: inc, knit to last 2 sts, inc, k1.

Rows 33, 41 and 45: inc, knit to end.

Cont without shaping until work measures 19(19:20)cm
(7½(7½:8)in), ending with a knit row.

Shape armhole

Cast off 5(6:7) sts, work to end.

Work ** to ** as on Left Front reversing shoulder
shaping.

SLEEVES (make 2)

Using 2¾mm (US 2) needles, cast on 55(57:59) sts and
work 2.5cm (1in) in k1, p1 rib.

Change to 3¼mm (US 3) needles and st st.

Inc each end of next and every foll 6th row to

95(99:103) sts.

Cont without shaping until work measures 46cm (18in),
ending with a purl row.

Shape sleevehead

Cast off 5(6:7) sts beg next 2 rows.

Dec each end of next 4 rows.

Dec each end of next and every foll alt row to 49 sts.

Dec each end of next 4 rows.

Cast off 3 sts beg next 4 rows.

Cast off.

EDGING

Using 2¾mm (US 2) needles, cast on 9 sts and work in
k1, p1 rib until the edging fits around the lower back, up
the front, across the back neck and down the other
front to the starting point, approximately 204cm (80in).
Cast off.

FINISHING

Join shoulder and side seams. Join sleeve seams. Ease
sleevehead into armhole and stitch into position. Ease
and pin edging into place around garment making sure
that it lies flat and the join is at the side seam. Stitch
into place.

Striped socks

PICTURED ON PAGE 54

SIZE

	Small	Medium	Large
foot length cm (in)	23 (9)	24 (9½)	25 (10)

MATERIALS

Rowan 4-ply Botany 50g balls:

mocha (M)	2	2	2
strawberry (C)	1	1	1

1 set each 4 x 3¼mm (US 3) and 4 x 4mm (US 6) double-ended needles

TENSION

24 sts and 28 rows = 10cm (4in) square over st st using Rowan 4-ply Botany and 4mm (US 6) needles.

ABBREVIATIONS

See page 67.

SOCKS (make 2)

Using 3¼mm (US 3) needles and C, cast on 22 sts on each of 3 needles. 66 sts.

Work as folls:

Round 1: using C, *k1, p1; rep from * to end.

Round 2-3: using M, *k1, p1; rep from * to end.

Round 4: as round 1.

Rep rounds 1-4 until work measures approximately 16cm (6¼in), ending with round 3. Change to 4mm (US 6) needles and cont in M only.

Next round: *k1, k2tog; rep from * to end. 44 sts.

Knit 9 rounds.

Work heel

Row 1: k11, turn.

Row 2: sl1, p21, turn. Leave rem 22 sts on spare needle.

Row 3: sl1, k20, turn.

Row 4: sl1, p19, turn.

Row 5: sl1, k18, turn.

Row 6: sl1, p17, turn.

Rows 7-14: work as set, placing marker each end of row 14.

Row 15: sl1, k9.

Row 16: sl1, p10.

Row 17: sl1, k11.

Row 18: sl1, p12.

Rows 19-26: work as set.

Row 27: sl1, k22, cont in round, knitting all sts. 44 sts. Cont in rounds until work, measured from heel marker, is 18(19:20)cm (7(7½:8)in).

Work toe

Round 1: k9, k2tog, sl1, k1, psso, k18, k2tog, sl1, k1, psso, k9.

Round 2: knit.

Round 3: k8, k2tog, sl1, k1, psso, k16, k2tog, sl1, k1, psso, k8.

Round 4: knit.

Round 5: k7, k2tog, sl1, k1, psso, k14, k2tog, sl1, k1, psso, k7.

Rounds 6-14: dec as set.

Round 15: cast off.

FINISHING

Join toe seam. Weave in any loose ends.

Chequered scarf

PICTURED ON PAGE 54

SIZE

92cm (36in) long and 18cm (7in) wide.

MATERIALS

Rowan 4-ply Botany 50g balls:

mocha (A)   2

strawberry (B)   1

1 pair each 3¼mm (US 3) and 3¾mm (US 5) needles

Spare needle

TENSION

1 patt rep = 2.5cm (1in) wide using Rowan 4-ply Botany
and 3¾mm (US 5) needles.

ABBREVIATIONS

See page 67.

SCARF (make 2)

Using 3¾mm (US 5) needles and B, cast on 59 sts
and work as folls:

Change to A.

Rows 1-3: knit.

Row 4: purl.

Change to B.

Row 5: k1, *k3, sl3p; rep from * to last 4 sts, k4.

Row 6: p1, *p3, sl3p; rep from * to last 4 sts, p4.

Row 7: k1, *k4, sl1p, k1; rep from * to last 4 sts, k4.

Row 8: p1, *p4, sl1p, p1; rep from * to last 4 sts, p4.

Change to A.

Row 9: k1, *sl3p, k3; rep from * to last 4 sts, sl3p, k1.

Row 10: p1, *sl3p, p3; rep from * to last 4 sts,
sl3p, p1.

Row 11: k1, *k1, sl1p, k4; rep from * to last 4 sts, k1,
sl1p, k2.

Row 12: p1, *p1, sl1p, p4; rep from * to last 4 sts,
p1, sl1p, p2.

Rows 5-12 form patt rep. Cont in patt until work
measures 20cm (8in).

Change to 3¼mm (US 3), A and k1, p1 rib.

Cont until work measures 46cm (18in).

Leave sts on spare needle.

FINISHING

Graft the two pieces of scarf together by placing RS
together. Then cast off by knitting together 1 st from
each piece. Weave in any loose ends.

Tyrolean cardigan

PICTURED ON PAGE 56

SIZES

	Small	Medium	Large
to fit bust (cm)	81-86	88-91	94-96
to fit bust (in)	(32-34)	(35-36)	(37-38)
actual size	91 (36)	96 (38)	102 (40)
back length	53 (21)	53 (21)	53 (21)
sleeve seam	44 (17½)	44 (17½)	44 (17½)

MATERIALS

Rowan wool cotton 50g balls:

deepest olive	11	11	12

Yarn for embroidery: flower, citron, riviera

1 pair each 3¼mm (US 3) and 4mm (US 6) needles

7 buttons

TENSION

22 sts and 30 rows = 10cm (4in) square over st st
using Rowan wool cotton and 4mm (US 6) needles.

ABBREVIATIONS

See page 67.

mb = k1, p1, k1, p1 into next st, turn, p4, turn, k4,
then take 2nd, 3rd and 4th sts over first st.

BACK

Using 3¼mm (US 3) needles, cast on 92(98:104) sts
and work 5cm (2in) in k2, p2 rib.

Change to 4mm (US 6) needles and st st.

Inc each end of 11th and every foll 16th row to
98(104:110) sts.

Cont without shaping until work measures 32cm
(12½in), ending with a purl row.

Shape armholes

Cast off 3(4:5) sts beg next 2 rows.

Dec each end next 4 rows.

Dec each end of next and every foll alt row to 78(82:86)
sts.

Cont without shaping until work measures 51cm (20in),
ending with a purl row.

Shape shoulders and neck

Rows 1-2: cast off 5 sts, patt to end.

Row 3: cast off 5 sts, patt 14(15:16), cast off
30(32:34) sts, patt to end.

Row 4: cast off 5 sts, patt to end.

Row 5: cast off 2 sts, patt to end.

Row 6: cast off 5 sts, patt to end.

Row 7: cast off 2 sts, patt to end.

Row 8: cast off.

Rejoin yarn to rem sts at neck edge and work
rows 5-8 again.

LEFT FRONT

Using 3¼mm (US 3) needles, cast on 44(48:52) sts and
work 5cm (2in) in k2, p2 rib.

Change to 4mm (US 6) needles and patt as folls:

Row 1: k15(17:19), mb, k5, mb, k9, mb, k5, mb,
k6(8:10).

Row 2: purl.

Row 3: k18(20:22), mb, kl5, mb, k9(11:13).

Row 4: purl.

Rows 1-4 form patt rep.

Cont in patt, inc beg of 16th and every foll 10th row to
50(54:58) sts.

Cont without shaping until work measures 32cm
(12½in), ending with a purl row.

Shape armhole

Cast off 3(4:5) sts, work to end.

Dec armhole edge on next 4 rows.

Dec armhole edge on next and every foll alt row to
40(43:46) sts.

Cont without shaping until work is 15 rows less than
Back to shoulder shaping, ending with a knit row.

Shape neck

Cast off 7(9:11) sts, patt to end.

Dec neck edge on next 6 rows.

Dec neck edge on next and every foll alt row to
23(24:25) sts, ending with a purl row.

Shape shoulder

Row 1: cast off 5 sts, patt to last 2 sts, k2tog.

Row 2: purl.

Rows 3-6: work as rows 1-2 twice.

Row 7: cast off.

RIGHT FRONT

Work as for Left Front reversing all shapings and noting:

Row 1: k6(8:10), mb, k5, mb, k9, mb, k5, mb, k15(17:19).

Row 3: k9(11:13), mb, k15, mb, k18(20:22).

EMBROIDERY

It is easier to embroider the fronts before finishing the garment (see diagram for embroidery).

SLEEVES

Using 3¼mm (US 3) needles, cast on 52(52:56) sts and work 5cm (2in) in k2, p2 rib, inc at end of last row. 53(53:57) sts.

Change to 4mm (US 6) needles and patt as folls:

Row 1: k23(23:25), mb, k5, mb, k23(23:25).

Row 2: purl.

Row 3: k26(26:28), mb, k26(26:28).

Row 4: purl.

Rows 1-4 form patt rep, inc each end of 5th and every foll 10th row to 75(77:79) sts, working extra sts in st st. Cont without shaping until work measures 44cm (17½in), ending with a purl row.

Shape sleevehead

Cast off 3(4:5) sts beg next 2 rows.

Dec each end next 4 rows.

Dec each end of next and every foll alt row to 41 sts.

Dec each end of next 4 rows.

Cast off 3 sts beg next 4 rows.

Cast off.

BUTTONBAND

Using 3¼mm (US 3) needles, cast on 7 sts and work 47cm (18½in) in k1, p1 rib, ending with a WS row. Leave on spare needle.

Mark positions for 6 buttons, the first 1cm (½in) from the bottom edge, the 2nd at 5cm (2in), the 6th 7cm (3in) from the top and the 3rd, 4th and 5th evenly spaced between the 2nd and 6th.

BUTTONHOLE BAND

Work as for buttonband, making buttonholes to match marked button positions.

Make buttonhole

Row 1 (RS): rib 3, cast off 1 st, rib to end.

Row 2: rib 3, yo, rib 3.

Do not break yarn.

NECKBAND

Join shoulder seams.

With RS facing and using 3¼mm (US 3) needles, rib across buttonhole band, pick up and knit 25(26:27) sts from right front neck, 39(41:43) sts from back neck, 25(26:27) sts from left front neck and rib across buttonband.

Work 5 rows in k1, p1 rib, making 7th buttonhole in rows 2 and 3.

Cast off.

FINISHING

Join side seams and sleeve seams. Ease sleevehead into armhole, stitch into place.

Attach buttonband and buttonhole band.

Sew on buttons.

Weave in loose ends.

Key

	Stitch	Colour
Petals	lazy daisy	flower
Centre	french knot	citron
Leaf	lazy daisy	riviera
Stem	stem stitch	riviera

Long-sleeved sweater with fairisle borders

PICTURED ON PAGE 58

SIZES

	Small	Medium	Large
to fit bust cm (in)	81 (32)	86 (34)	91 (36)
actual size	86 (34)	91 (36)	96 (38)
back length	51 (20)	51 (20)	53 (21)
sleeve seam	46 (18)	46 (18)	46 (18)

MATERIALS

Rowan 4-ply cotton 50g balls:

violet (M)	7	8	8

For all sizes, Rowan 4-ply cotton 50g balls: 1 ball each marine, olive, aegean and fandango

1 pair each 2¾mm (US 2) and 3¼mm (US 3) needles

Stitch holder

TENSION

26 sts and 36 rows = 10cm (4in) square over st st using Rowan 4-ply cotton and 3¼mm (US 3) needles.

ABBREVIATIONS

See page 67.

BACK

Using 2¾mm (US 2) needles and M, cast on 99(107:115) sts and work 6cm (2½in) in k1, p1 rib.

Change to 3¼mm (US 3) needles and st st and work 26 rows from chart.

Cont in M only, inc each end of next and every foll 8th row to 109(117:125) sts

Cont until work measures 29(29:32)cm (11½(11½:12½)in), ending with a WS row.

Shape armholes

Cast off 4(5:6) sts beg next 2 rows.

Dec at each end of next 4 rows.

Dec each end of next and every foll alt row to 85(91:97) sts.

Cont until work measures 48(48:51)cm (19(19:20)in), ending with a WS row.

Shape shoulders and neck

Cast off 4 sts beg next 4 rows.

Row 5: cast off 4 sts, patt 14(16:18) sts, cast off 33(35:37) sts, patt to end.

Row 6: cast off 4 sts, patt to end.

Row 7: cast off 3 sts, patt to end.

Row 8: cast off 4 sts, patt to end.

Row 9: cast off 2 sts, patt to end.

Row 10: cast off.

Rejoin yarn to rem sts at neck edge.

Work rows 7-10 again.

FRONT

Work as Back until work measures 43(43:45)cm (17(17:17¾)in), ending with a WS row.

Shape neck

Row 1: k33(35:37), turn.

Working on these 33(35:37) sts:

**Rows 2-13: dec neck edge. 21(23:25) sts.

Cont without shaping until work measures same as Back at shoulder, ending at armhole edge.

Shape shoulder

Cast off 4 sts beg next and foll 3 alt rows

Work 1 row.

Cast off.

Place 19(21:23) sts on holder.

Rejoin yarn to rem sts at neck edge, work to end.

Work from ** to end.

SLEEVES (make 2)

Using 2¾mm (US 2) needles and M, cast on 55(57:59) sts and work 5cm (2in) in k1, p1 rib.

Change to 3¼mm (US 3) needles and st st and work 26 rows from chart.

Cont in M only, inc each end of 7th and every foll 6th row to 89(91:93) sts, making fully fashioned incs by k2, inc, work to last 4 sts, inc, k3.

Cont without shaping until work measures 46cm (18in), ending with a WS row.

Shape sleevehead

Cast off 4(5:6) sts beg next 2 rows.

Dec each end of next 4 rows.

Dec each end of next and every foll alt row to 51 sts.

Dec each end of next 6 rows.

Cast off 3 sts beg next 4 rows.

Cast off.

NECKBAND

Join right shoulder seam.

With RS facing and using 2¾mm (US 2) needles and M,

pick up and knit 22 sts from side front neck, k19(21:23)

sts from holder, pick up and knit 22 sts from side front

neck and 43(45:47) sts from back neck.

Work 2cm (½in) in k1, p1 rib

Cast off loosely.

FINISHING

Join left shoulder seam and neckband. Join side seams.

Join sleeve seams. Ease sleevehead into armhole and

stitch into place. Weave in any loose ends.

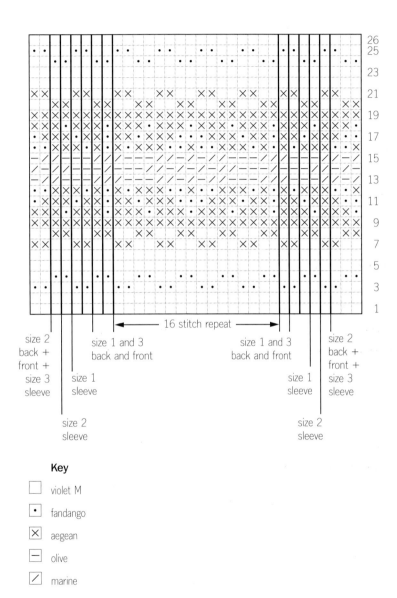

Key

☐ violet M

• fandango

☒ aegean

— olive

╱ marine

Beaded sweater

PICTURED ON PAGE 60

SIZES

	Small	Medium	Large
to fit bust cm (in)	81 (32)	86 (34)	91 (36)
actual size	86 (34)	91 (36)	96 (38)
back length	51 (20)	51 (20)	51 (20)
sleeve seam	4 (1½)	4 (1½)	4 (1½)

MATERIALS

Rowan 4-ply Botany 50g balls:

chrome	4	5	5

900 beads.

1 pair each 2¾mm (US 2) needles and 3¼mm (US 3) needles.

TENSION

28 sts and 36 rows = 10cm (4in) square over st st using Rowan 4-ply Botany and 3¼mm (US 3) needles.

ABBREVIATIONS

See page 67.

MB = move a bead to the front of the slipped stitch

NOTE

Thread 300 beads on to each of 3 balls of yarn.

BACK

Using 2¾mm (US 2) needles and a ball of yarn without beads, cast on 111(117:129) sts and work 5cm (2in) in k1, p1 rib.

Break yarn.

Change to 3¼mm (US 3) needles and join in ball of yarn with beads and work as folls:

Rows 1-4: st st.

Row 5: k4, *yf, sl1p, MB, yb, k5; rep from * ending last rep k4.

Rows 6-12: st st, inc each end of row 11.

Row 13: k2, *yf, sl1p, MB, yb, k5; rep from * ending last rep k2.

Rows 14-16: st st.

Rows 1-16 set the bead patt.

Keeping patt correct, inc each end of rows 5 and 15 in the next rep and every foll 10th row to 121(127:135) sts, working extra sts into patt.

Cont without shaping until work measures 29cm (11½in), ending with a WS row.

Shape raglan armholes

Rows 1-2: cast off 8(9:10) sts, patt to end.

Row 3: dec each end.

Row 4: purl.

Keeping patt correct, rep rows 3-4 to 81(85:91) sts.

Shape neck

Next row (RS): dec, patt 18(19:21), cast off 41(43:45) sts, patt 18(19:21), dec.

On 19(20:22) sts:

Work 1 row.

Dec each end of next and every alt row until 3(2:2) sts rem.

Next row: p3(2:2)tog. Fasten off.

Rejoin yarn to rem sts and work to match.

FRONT

Work as for Back.

SLEEVES (make 2)

Using 2¾mm (US 2) needles, cast on 83(85:87) sts and work 5 rows in k1, p1 rib.

Row 6: rib 0(1:2), *rib 3, inc; rep from * 20 times, rib 3(4:5). 103(105:107) sts.

Change to 3¼mm (US 3) needles and patt 8 rows as on Back noting row 5: k3(4:5), *yf, sl1p, MB, yb, k5; rep from * ending last rep k3(4:5).

Shape raglan sleeve top

Rows 9-10: cast off 8(9:10) sts beg each row.

Keeping patt correct as on Back, dec each end of next and every foll alt row to 47(45:41) sts.

Cast off.

NECKBAND

Join raglan sleeve seams to front and right back.

With RS facing and using 2¾mm (US 2) needles, pick up and knit *47(45:41) sts across left sleeve, 17(17:18) sts down side front, 41(43:45) sts across centre front, 17(17:18) sts up side front; rep from * to * for right sleeve and back.

Work 5 rows in k1, p1 rib.

Cast off.

FINISHING

Join neckband and last raglan seam. Join side and sleeve seams. Weave in any loose ends.

Long-sleeved fairisle sweater

PICTURED ON PAGE 62

SIZES

	Small	Medium	Large
to fit bust cm (in)	81 (32)	86 (34)	91 (36)
actual size	86 (34)	91 (36)	96 (38)
back length	50 (19¾)	50 (19¾)	53 (21)
sleeve seam	46 (18)	46 (18)	46 (18)

MATERIALS

Rowan Cotton glacé 50g balls:

poppy (M)	7	8	8
candy floss (C)	1	2	2
passion	1	1	1
bud	1	2	2
reef	1	1	1
hyacinth	1	2	2

1 pair each 3mm (US 2) and 3¾mm (US 5) needles

TENSION

25 sts and 30 rows = 10cm (4in) square over patt using Rowan Cotton glacé and 3¾mm (US 5) needles.

ABBREVIATIONS

See page 67.

BACK

Using 3mm (US 2) needles and M, cast on 107(113:119) sts and work 6cm (2½in) in k1, p1 rib. Change to 3¾mm (US 5) needles, st st and foll chart until work measures 29(29:32)cm (11½(11½:12½)in), ending with a WS row. Note chart row.

Shape armholes

Cast off 4(5:6) sts beg next 2 rows.

Dec each end next 4 rows.

Dec each end of next and every foll alt row to 85(89:93) sts.

Cont without shaping until work measures 48(48:51)cm (19(19:20)in), ending with a WS row. Note chart row.

Shape shoulders and neck

Rows 1-2: cast off 6 sts, patt to end.

Row 3: cast off 6 sts, patt 17(18:19), cast off 27(29:31) sts, patt to end.

Working on 23(24:25) sts:

Row 4: cast off 6 sts, patt to end.

Row 5: cast off 3 sts, patt to end.

Row 6: work as row 4.

Row 7: cast off 2 sts, patt to end.

Row 8: cast off.

Rejoin yarns to rem sts at neck edge and work rows 5-8 again.

FRONT

Work as Back until work is 13 rows less than Back to shoulder shaping, ending with a RS row.

Shape neck

Row 1 (WS): patt 34(35:36), cast off 17(19:21) sts, patt to end.

Working on these 34(35:36) sts:

Rows 2-7: dec neck edge, patt.

Rows 8-13: dec neck edge on alt rows, patt, ending with a WS row. 25(26:27) sts.

Shape shoulder

Row 14: cast off 6 sts, patt to last 2 sts, dec.

Row 15: patt.

Rows 16-19: cast off 6 sts beg of alt rows.

Row 20: cast off.

Rejoin yarns to rem sts at neck edge and work to match.

SLEEVES (make 2)

Using 3mm (US 2) needles and M, cast on 55(57:59) sts and work 5cm (2in) in k1, p1 rib.

Change to 3¾mm (US 5) needles, st st and foll chart, starting 14 rows before noted chart row at Back armhole shaping to match patts at armhole.

Inc each end of 5th and every foll 5th row to 93(95:97) sts, working extra sts into patt. Cont without shaping until work measures approximately 46cm (18in), ending on same chart row before Back armhole shaping.

Shape sleevehead

Cast off 4(5:6) sts beg next 2 rows. Dec each end of
next 4 rows.

Dec each end of next and every foll alt row to 53 sts.

Dec each end of next 8 rows.

Cast off 4 sts beg next 4 rows.

Cast off.

COLLAR

Using 3mm (US 2) needles and C, cast on 147 sts.

Change to M and knit 1 row.

Work as folls:

Row 2: *k1, p1; rep from * to last st, k1.

Row 3: p1, k1, p1, sl1, p1, psso, rib to last 5 sts,
k2tog, p1, k1, p1.

Row 4: k1, p1, k1, p2, rib to last 5 sts, p2, k1, p1, k1.

Row 5: p1, k1, p1, sl1, k1, psso, rib to last 5 sts,
k2tog, p1, k1, p1.

Rep rows 2-5 until 121 sts rem.

Cast off.

FINISHING

Weave in any loose ends. Join shoulder, side and sleeve
seams. Ease sleevehead into armhole and stitch into
place. Place RS of collar to WS of sweater, joining collar
at centre front neck (see photograph on page 62). Ease
collar around neck and stitch in position.

Key

☐ poppy

⊙ candyfloss

Ⅴ passion

• bud

╱ reef

☒ hyacinth

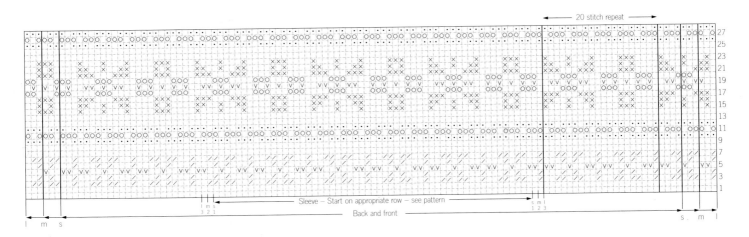

Author's acknowledgments

My warmest thanks to all the people who have contributed to this book, for their enthusiasm, encouragement and commitment:

Chris Bacon, Yesterknits; Rosemary Harden, Keeper of Collections, Museum of Costume, Bath; Stephen Sheard and Eva Yates.

Kate, Kathleen, Kim, Anne and Lyndsay at Rowan, Gill Everett and her team of knitters, Marilyn Wilson, Lillan Dodd, Tomoko and Eleanor.

Catherine Gratwicke, Francine Kay, Denise Bates, Emma Callery, Helen Brocklehurst, Georgina Rhodes and James Dallas.

To Lisa Pendreigh for the original concept.

And especially to my family for their constant support and endless patience.

The author and publisher would like to thank the following people and companies for their help with this book: Yesterknits Archive, Edinburgh and the Museum of Costume, Bath for the use of their patterns; Rowan and Jaeger Yarns for supplying yarn for the garments and Karl Donaghue Tel: 020 8466 1233, Emma Hope Tel: 020 7259 9566, Jigsaw Tel: 020 7491 4244, Cath Kidston Tel: 020 7221 4000, Orla Kiely Tel: 020 7585 3322, Tab Tel: 01273 821448, The Cross Tel: 020 7727 6760 for loaning props for photography.

Yarn stockists

The patterns in this book use Rowan and Jaeger yarns; to find your nearest supplier call the appropriate number given below. If you decide to use a substitute yarn, calculate the number of balls required by the number of metres per ball rather than by the yarn weight.

Please note that after October 2002 Rowan True 4-ply used in some of the patterns should be substituted by Rowan 4-ply Soft or Jaeger MM DK.

UNITED KINGDOM
(Head Office): Green Lane Mill, Holmfirth, West Yorkshire, Tel: (44) (0) 1484 681881. Email: mail@knitrowan.com

AUSTRALIA
Australian Country Spinners, 314 Albert Street, Brunswick, Victoria 3056 Tel: (03) 9380 3801

BELGIUM
Pavan, Koningin Astridlaan 78, B9000 Gent. Tel: (32) 9 221 8591

DENMARK
Please contact Rowan for Stockist details.

FRANCE
Elle Tricot: 8 Rue du Coq, 67000 Strasbourg. Tel: (33) 3 88 23 03 13.

GERMANY
Wolle & Design, Wolfshovener Strasse 76, 52428 Julich-Stetternich. Tel: (49) 2461 54735.

HOLLAND
de Afstap, Oude Leliestraat 12, 1015 AW Amsterdam. Tel: (31) 20 6231445.

HONG KONG
East Unity Co Ltd, Unit B2, 7/F., Block B, Kailey Industrial Centre, 12 Fung Yip Street, Chai Wan. Tel: (852) 2869 7110.

ICELAND
Storkurinn, Kjorgardi, Laugavegi 59, Reykjavik. Tel: (354) 551 82 58.

JAPAN (Rowan only) DiaKeito Co Ltd, 2-3-11 Senba-Higashi, Minoh City, Osaka. Tel: (81) 727 27 6604.

JAPAN (Jaeger only) Puppy Co Ltd, TOC Building, 7-22-17 Nishigotanda, Shinagawa-ku, Tokyo. Tel: (81) 3 3494 2395.

NEW ZEALAND
Please contact Rowan for Stockist details.

SWEDEN (Rowan only)
Wincent: Norrtulsgaten 65, 11345 Stockholm. Tel: (46) 8 673 70 60.